# HEAVENLY HUMOR

## for the

# Dad's Soul

75 Inspirational Readings from Fellow Fathers
(and Those Who Love Them)

# HEAVENLY HUMOR

for the

# Dad's Soul

75 Inspirational Readings from Fellow Fathers
(and Those Who Love Them)

BARBOUR
PUBLISHING

# CONTENTS

## Section 1—It Ain't Easy (Being a Dad): Character

Need a Pencil? We've Got Some! . . . . . . . . . . . . . . 10
Beauty Killed the Beast? . . . . . . . . . . . . . . . . . . . . 13
Watch Your Tongue . . . . . . . . . . . . . . . . . . . . . . . 16
When a Daughter Gets Behind the Wheel . . . . . . . 19
Taking Care of Business . . . . . . . . . . . . . . . . . . . . 22
Problem Solving . . . . . . . . . . . . . . . . . . . . . . . . . 25

## Section 2—A Place for All Dads: Relationships

If It Ain't Broke, Don't Break It . . . . . . . . . . . . . . 30
Can Anyone Say, "Amen"? . . . . . . . . . . . . . . . . . . 33
A Place for Everything . . . . . . . . . . . . . . . . . . . . . 36
Easier to Be a Philistine . . . . . . . . . . . . . . . . . . . . 39
Using Someone Else's Gifts . . . . . . . . . . . . . . . . . . 42

## Section 3—Chillaxin' with the Ultimate Father: Inner Life

My Thumb-Sucking Theology . . . . . . . . . . . . . . . . 46
Where Are You? . . . . . . . . . . . . . . . . . . . . . . . . . 49
All in the Family . . . . . . . . . . . . . . . . . . . . . . . . . 52
The Road to Euro Disney . . . . . . . . . . . . . . . . . . . 55
We Really Belong to Each Other . . . . . . . . . . . . . . 58
How Many Bads Make a Good? . . . . . . . . . . . . . . 61
It Hurts Me More . . . . . . . . . . . . . . . . . . . . . . . . 64

## SECTION 4—THE DAD POWERHOUSE 1: GOD'S RESCUE

Annoying Questions . . . . . . . . . . . . . . . . . . . . . . . . . 68
Our King of the Jungle . . . . . . . . . . . . . . . . . . . . . 71
Step Relocation . . . . . . . . . . . . . . . . . . . . . . . . . . . 74
There's Little Sitting in Babysitting . . . . . . . . . . . . 77
Thou Shalt Not Kill . . . . . . . . . . . . . . . . . . . . . . . 80
Fried Chicken . . . . . . . . . . . . . . . . . . . . . . . . . . . . 83
Those Difficult Questions . . . . . . . . . . . . . . . . . . . 86

## SECTION 5—A DAD'S GOTTA BE HAPPY: PEACE

Afraid of the . . . . . . . . . . . . . . . . . . . . . . . . . . . . . 90
It's the Taking Part That Counts . . . . . . . . . . . . . . 93
If One Picture's Worth a Thousand Words . . . . . . . 96
Problem Solving the Manly Way . . . . . . . . . . . . . . 99
Took an Attitude . . . . . . . . . . . . . . . . . . . . . . . . . 102

## SECTION 6—DOIN' THE DAD BOOGIE: CELEBRATION

Golf . . . . . . . . . . . . . . . . . . . . . . . . . . . . . . . . . . . 106
Father's Day in Church (An Extravagant
    Exaggeration) . . . . . . . . . . . . . . . . . . . . . . . . . 109
I Am Soooo Tired . . . . . . . . . . . . . . . . . . . . . . . . 112
Blessed Annoyance . . . . . . . . . . . . . . . . . . . . . . . 115
Honor, Dedication, and Peas . . . . . . . . . . . . . . . . 118
When You Were Just Like Us . . . . . . . . . . . . . . . . 121

## SECTION 7—WHO'S THE MAN?: TRUSTING GOD

Money, Money, Money . . . . . . . . . . . . . . . . . . . . 126

A+ for Abraham . . . . . . . . . . . . . . . . . . . . . . . . . . . 129

Bad Hair Day . . . . . . . . . . . . . . . . . . . . . . . . . . . . . 132

Pine Tree Ouch Fest . . . . . . . . . . . . . . . . . . . . . . . 135

Answer in the Form of a Question. . . . . . . . . . . . 138

My Sweet Time . . . . . . . . . . . . . . . . . . . . . . . . . . . 141

Short-Term Mysteries . . . . . . . . . . . . . . . . . . . . . . 144

# Section 8—Who Does a Dad Follow?: Letting Jesus Lead

Dadzilla. . . . . . . . . . . . . . . . . . . . . . . . . . . . . . . . . 148

My (Son's) Hero. . . . . . . . . . . . . . . . . . . . . . . . . . . 151

Prejudiced . . . . . . . . . . . . . . . . . . . . . . . . . . . . . . . 154

Dads of Deuteronomy. . . . . . . . . . . . . . . . . . . . . . 156

Follow the Leader . . . . . . . . . . . . . . . . . . . . . . . . . 159

The Next Generation. . . . . . . . . . . . . . . . . . . . . . . 162

Hardheaded . . . . . . . . . . . . . . . . . . . . . . . . . . . . . 165

Job's Job. . . . . . . . . . . . . . . . . . . . . . . . . . . . . . . . . 168

Finding Joy under the Sun. . . . . . . . . . . . . . . . . . . 171

# Section 9—Leaning on Abba's Arms: God's Protection

A Lesson in Laying Carpet . . . . . . . . . . . . . . . . . . 176

Jelly Belly Baby . . . . . . . . . . . . . . . . . . . . . . . . . . . 179

Re: Tim's Brief Career as a Pianist . . . . . . . . . . . . 182

How Do You Measure Success? . . . . . . . . . . . . . . 185

Where Do I Begin? . . . . . . . . . . . . . . . . . . . . . . . . 188

The Cake Auction . . . . . . . . . . . . . . . . . . . . . . . . . 191

Now Get to Sleep! . . . . . . . . . . . . . . . . . . . . . . . . . 194

Papa Bear's in Good Hands . . . . . . . . . . . . . . . . . . 197

Recognizing the Problem. . . . . . . . . . . . . . . . . . . . 200

## Section 10—Dad-ology 101: Making Memories

Let Them Come . . . . . . . . . . . . . . . . . . . . . . . . . . 204
So Many Books, So Little Sleep. . . . . . . . . . . . . . 207
Fish Oil—the Nectar of Life . . . . . . . . . . . . . . . . 210
Get Your Hands Dirty. . . . . . . . . . . . . . . . . . . . . . 213
"Father" Not "Friend" . . . . . . . . . . . . . . . . . . . . . 216
Daddy Day Care . . . . . . . . . . . . . . . . . . . . . . . . . . 218
Teenagers! . . . . . . . . . . . . . . . . . . . . . . . . . . . . . . . 221

## Section 11—The Dad Powerhouse 2: Connecting to God

Who Is That Guy?. . . . . . . . . . . . . . . . . . . . . . . . . 224
A Parable about Radish Seeds . . . . . . . . . . . . . . . 227
Twenty-First-Century Communication Is
  Old School. . . . . . . . . . . . . . . . . . . . . . . . . . . . . 230
History-Making . . . . . . . . . . . . . . . . . . . . . . . . . . 233
We Could Have Named Him Storm . . . . . . . . . . 236
The Good New Days. . . . . . . . . . . . . . . . . . . . . . . 239
The Dogwood Tree . . . . . . . . . . . . . . . . . . . . . . . . 242

# It Ain't Easy (Being a Dad): Character

*My father gave me the greatest gift anyone could give another person, he believed in me.*
JIM VALVANO

# Need a Pencil?
# We've Got Some!

Gayle Lintz

*There is a time for everything, and a season
for every activity under the heavens. . .
a time to keep and a time to throw away.*
Ecclesiastes 3:1, 6 niv

The only kind of "golf" I ever played was the miniature kind. But I do know what real golfers do to document their games. They get a score card and a little pencil at the beginning of every game. They carefully write down their scores for each hole. At the end of the game, they add up those scores, compare them with their friends, then throw those little pencils away. Most golfers do that. Not my dad.

My dad played golf every Saturday morning all my growing up years. And, every Saturday, he brought home his little pencil. After his retirement, he played golf on Tuesday and Friday mornings. Then he was bringing home *two* little pencils every week.

My mother found all these pencils annoying, as they

began to fill up drawers. My dad was persistent. These were perfectly good, solid wooden pencils! And indeed they were. Except that, as they wore down and needed sharpening, they became so short that only toddlers could easily hold them to write. Still, he kept bringing them home.

A few months after my mom passed away, Dad moved to a retirement residence. We went through the house, preparing for an estate sale. We found little golf pencils everywhere.

We found them in the desk drawers, sometimes in boxes and drawer organizers, but sometimes just slid in between pens and regular pencils and rulers.

In the garage, we found Sir Walter Raleigh tobacco cans (kept from years earlier, when he smoked a pipe) crammed full of pencils. They were laid end-to-end in cheese boxes. On shelves in his garage workroom, every manner of container held little golf pencils.

We gathered up most of them and put them on the table with the estate sale cashbox. When shoppers came to pay, we pointed to the pencils. "Please, take some," we said. "Oh, no thanks," some shoppers said. "Really," we said, intently. "We insist."

A golf pencil collector spied the box. In addition to the plain yellow pencils, a few were different colors and some had the names of golf courses around the country where Dad had played during vacations.

"I can take these to conventions and trade them," the collector explained. He spent about an hour sifting through the box. I don't know how many he chose, but he insisted on giving us a couple of dollars for them.

My dad enjoyed all the seasons of his life. He enjoyed working and traveling, photography and coin collecting. He enjoyed his wife, his family, and his golf. He enjoyed keeping all his little golf pencils. Our memories of Dad were secure. We have kept and cherished them. But we could get rid of the little golf pencils. And we liked knowing that sharing his pencil collection gave such joy to a fellow enthusiast.

# Beauty Killed the Beast?

## Paul Muckley

*"You give a tenth of your spices—mint, dill and cumin.*
*But you have neglected the more important matters*
*of the law—justice, mercy and faithfulness.*
*You should have practiced the latter,*
*without neglecting the former."*

MATTHEW 23:23 NIV

Quick: What is the eighth wonder of the world?

Let's see. . .I think the first seven include the pyramids of Egypt, the hanging gardens of Babylon, the Great Wall of China, and the Los Angeles freeway. And maybe professional sports in Cleveland.

But the eighth wonder of the world—so says the main character in the film—is King Kong.

If you're not familiar with *King Kong*, it's an old movie. Really old. 1933 old. So old, we thought it might be safe viewing for our four-year-old son. And apart from all the machine guns and human sacrifice, it was great.

The story in a nutshell: Down-on-his-luck producer

takes down-on-her-luck actress to down-on-its-luck mystery island. Honkin' big ape falls for actress. Producer gasses ape. Ape creates mayhem in New York City. Four-year-old boy is fascinated.

In the film's climax, Kong has carried his lovely and beloved Fay Wray up the side of the Empire State Building. Ultimately, he'll be buzzed by the most modern, fearsome weapon in the US military arsenal—the open-cockpit biplane. And though we all know he's just a guy in a monkey suit, it's kind of sad when the planes prevail and Kong goes crashing to the New York sidewalk.

When a city cop grabs the producer's shoulder and says, "Well Denham, the airplanes got him," the response is a Hollywood classic: "Oh no, it wasn't the airplanes—it was beauty killed the beast."

Hollywood classic or no, my son glanced up with a look of disbelief on his face. "Nuh-uh," he insisted, "it was the planes!"

Young kids are a pretty literal bunch—if you use a figure of speech, you'll likely confuse them. (I recall my little brother's horror when dad, describing the struggles of our town's high school basketball team, said the locals were ready to "crucify" the coach.) If you joke about a monster under the bed, young kids might just believe you. If you ask them to pick-up-the-toys-off-the-floor-of-their-room-and-put-them-all-back-where-they-belong. . .well, that's where "taking dad literally" usually breaks down.

As we grow up, we begin to understand nuance.

We learn when others speak literally, when they speak figuratively, and when they (too often) speak ignorantly. We realize when words are painting a bigger picture—just like Jesus indicated to those Pharisees and teachers of the law in Matthew 23.

It's great to *do* all the things God says. In Jesus' time and place, that included tithing, giving a tenth of their crops even down to the pickle spices.

But it's just as important to *be* the kind of person God wants, someone who's fair with others, lives by the Golden Rule, and follows Jesus consistently in good times or bad.

If the *do*ing overshadows the *be*ing, we're little better than a giant monkey on top of a skyscraper—drawing attention to ourselves, maybe, but vulnerable to those little biplanes of pride, arrogance, and unkindness.

That's when ugly kills the beast.

# WATCH YOUR TONGUE

## PAUL MUCKLEY

*Those who consider themselves religious and yet do not keep
a tight rein on their tongues deceive themselves,
and their religion is worthless.*

### JAMES 1:26 NIV

Nearly a month has passed, and evidence of the incident remains.

As I write, it's Valentine's Eve. (In my wife's mind, that extends the holiday—kind of like her "birth week.") The incident occurred in mid-January, on a bitterly cold, wishing-for-some-of-that-global-warming kind of Saturday morning.

What *was* the incident?

A murder? No, but there was blood.

A mugging? No, but there was trauma.

A UFO encounter? Maybe. . .some kind of alien, brain-sucking experiment seems a good possibility when an eight-year-old boy sticks his tongue to a frozen metal lamppost.

Oh, and that evidence. . .well, you can still see the

little triangular patch of skin that stayed behind when the kid moved on.

Ever see the movie *Dumb and Dumber*? Actor Jeff Daniels, portraying "Harry," pulls the same trick on a Colorado ski lift. Stuck fast, he rides around and around before finally mumbling to a seatmate, "Heeeey, kiiiidd. . .yoouu woouuldnn' haaappeenn tuhh haaave uh cuuup uhh waaaaahmm waaattttuuhh, wouulld yuhh?"

Too bad my son didn't have that presence of mind. But perhaps right then his mind was floating through the far reaches of space.

He has a story, though I don't entirely follow the logic: He was running away from the dog, then turned around and, whoa—his tongue was fused to a cold piece of iron! It would make more sense to me if the *dog* had gotten stuck, since canine tongues typically hang out much farther than boys'. But that's just my forty-five-year-old, fuddy-daddy perspective.

Dad had just stumbled out of bed and was putting a toothbrush in his mouth, when the boy stumbled into the bathroom, bleeding from *his* mouth.

Even early in the morning, when my eyes work as well as binoculars in gravy, I could see we had trouble.

"What happened to you?" I demanded.

"Ahblaah ubbluba amanabaaa," he answered.

"What?"

"Ahblaah ubbluba amanabaaa," he repeated. At least I think he repeated it. It was kind of hard to tell.

In time, like a TV crime scene investigator (though, sadly, not nearly as good-looking as most), I assembled the clues and determined the truth: My son's tongue had chosen the wrong moment, on the wrong day, at the wrong place, to do something crazy. Traumatic results followed.

(Wow, if I can't spin a spiritual truth from that, I don't deserve the $200,000 the publisher is paying for this piece.)

Oops, sorry. . .momentarily got to daydreaming there.

Seriously though, it's easier to yank your tongue off a frigid lamppost than to miss all the Bible's warnings about careless speech. Public enemy number one: the tongue.

We dads should be especially careful. An ill-advised comment can ruin a kid's day—and maybe lodge there for a lifetime.

Though he was discussing a Christian's witness to the world, the apostle Paul's rule in Colossians 4:6 (NIV) applies to fathers: "Let your conversation be always full of grace, seasoned with salt."

Salt adds flavor. Salt preserves. And salt melts the ice that troubles our tongues.

# WHEN A DAUGHTER GETS BEHIND THE WHEEL

PAUL M. MILLER

*You were once darkness,*
*but now you are light in the Lord.*
EPHESIANS 5:8 NIV

The day had arrived! Lisa was taking her on-the-road driving test after a semester of driver's ed classes. On a calendar in her room, my daughter had marked off every day leading up to that momentous occasion.

"Anything have you worried?" I asked her on the way over to the motor vehicle testing station.

"No, not really. I just can't wait to get behind this wheel."

I glanced over at her mother (this was a family moment). She looked a bit apprehensive. In the spirit of encouragement, I glossed over her obvious concern with, "We've been looking forward to this day, too, Lisa."

In the back of my mind, I recalled the couple of sessions I spent attempting to teach Lisa the rudiments of defensive driving. That's when I decided the school's driver's ed course was the way to go. *I'll let someone else grow prematurely gray,* I thought.

There's one moment still fresh in my mind. One afternoon, Lisa paid an unexpected visit to my office. "Dad, my driving instructor has gotten kind of upset teaching me to parallel park. . ."

"So you want to inflict the same punishment on me, too?"

"No, I just want you to calmly show me how to park next to a curb, that's all. Please?"

The next Saturday dawned bright and beautiful. We were in the church parking lot, where I'd set orange cones to represent the front and back of two parked cars. Patiently, I'd shown Lisa how to pull up next to the front car then swing back into the space without smashing the rear car's back fender. We must have maneuvered through the experience a half-dozen times. All that we achieved over the hour was a collection of squashed parking cones and a flood of Lisa's tears.

Eventually, Lisa went in to take the driving test again. Right before the test, she had this conversation with the tester:

"Sir?"

"Yes?"

"How many points do I lose if I can't parallel park?"

"Three."

"Okay then, please just subtract those points before we even start."

At our celebration supper after Lisa successfully

passed her road test (even with the subtraction of those three parking points), we all congratulated her and joked with her, calling her the "A.J. Hoyt of Knox Avenue."

Later, to make some kind of serious impression, I read this verse from Ephesians: "You were once darkness, but now you are light in the Lord" (Ephesians 5:8 NIV).

"What's that got to do with my driving?" asked Lisa.

"It means that you were definitely in darkness to driving, but now you are enlightened, so drive as a child of light."

Everyone around the table agreed. Of course, we didn't anticipate the evening Lisa would drive her brother's classic Buick Riviera through the garage wall into our family room. But that's a story for another time.

# Taking Care of Business

P. Reginald Legume

*The LORD God took the man and put him in the
Garden of Eden to work it and take care of it.*
GENESIS 2:15 NIV

I am a busy man. Busy doing *what*? Busy doing *this*, of course. How busy can someone who does "this" be, you ask? *If you only knew*, I would likely reply! For, much like yourself, I am under a tremendous amount of pressure each and every day.

But that's par for the course in the highly competitive man-world we dads live in. After all, we've been charged with the task of bringing home the big megabucks to feed and clothe our hungry families and provide them with the things they desperately need to live, grow, and lead a godly life, such as Netflix, a smartphone, and an Xbox 360.

In order to meet the needs of a large, modern family the average man now needs to work at least sixty hours a day, nine days a week. So, with the crushing weight of daily man-responsibility strapped to our aching backs like that poor guy in *Pilgrim's Progress*, I, like most dads, am often looking for a way to relax. And by relax I mean relax the way most of us dads relax: yard work, fixing things, etc.

This may seem like a daunting task, but without the strong leadership[1] a man can provide, the modern family would plummet helplessly into the abyss of moral laxity, spiritual turpitude,[2] and the total lack of a brand-new car[3] for each of our kids when they turn sixteen.

So, heigh-ho, it's off to work we go! Yes men, *there is no escape.* We've been strapped *forever* to the black cart of modern man-work, whipped relentlessly by the need to generate cash at just about the same rate the sun burns hydrogen.

So to help ease the burden of our grueling fate[4] I offer these ancient words of wisdom from that purveyor of godly horse sense—Mr. Ed.

Well, not exactly *the* Mr. Ed, but another horse of the talking variety from C. S. Lewis's novel *The Magician's Nephew.* Much like myself, this manly workhorse was grumbling about his fate to his beloved master, the Cabby.

*HORSE: Yes. Let me think now, let me think. Yes, you used to tie that horrid black thing behind me and then hit me to make me run, and however far I ran, this black thing would always be coming rattle-rattle behind me.*

---

1. From our hammocks, of course.
2. Which also removes paint.
3. With paid insurance!
4. After all, we're only spending *one week* in Hilton Head this summer.

*HORSE'S MASTER: We had our living to earn, see. Yours the same as mine. And if there 'adn't been no work and no whip ther'd 'ave been no stable, no hay, no mash, and no oats.*

Amen to that! Time to get back to work. . .

# Problem Solving

GAYLE LINTZ

*Listen, my sons, to a father's instruction;*
*pay attention and gain understanding.*
PROVERBS 4:1 NIV

My sister and her family moved from West Texas to Seattle one June several years ago. The children were seven, nine, and eleven. They loved the Northwest but were accustomed to the wide open dryness of San Angelo. When winter arrived, with afternoon darkness and constant drizzle, the kids were frustrated by not being able to play outdoors as much as they were used to. My brother-in-law took the complaining just so long, then he decided to alleviate the situation. He built them a climbing wall.

That may sound like a simple and reasonable solution, but they lived in an apartment complex and had no garage. He created the climbing wall down the hallway in the center of their unit. He purchased a dozen or so rock climbing wall handholds at the local sporting goods store. He drilled holes into the wall studs and attached

25

the handholds. He put them at various levels along the walls, at distances that were manageable for younger bodies. And that was that.

My nephews and niece were elated. The setup was perfect. It was an interesting solitary activity, working out how to get from one end of the hallway to the other, without touching any body part to the floor. It was challenging with two or three of them racing from end to end, working from wall to wall across the hall, around doorways, over and under siblings (and sometimes parents), to achieve wall-climbing success.

The children remained interested all winter and into the spring, creating games, trying new contests, honing their expertise. When the weather improved, they spent more time outdoors, but they never abandoned their indoor play apparatus.

In the summer, the family found a house to rent. Looking forward to more space indoors and out, they packed up quickly and got ready to move. My brother-in-law removed the handholds from the hallway walls, spackled up those holes (along with whatever dents and damage that feet, hands, and elbows had made), and applied a fresh coat of paint. The apartment was pristine, and the owners didn't notice anything amiss.

At their new home, a multi-level house, the children made up a new game—Bowling Pin Siblings—played on the several short staircases there. They were as inventive as their dad.

We all understand that listening to parents' instruction

is important. But, watching parents' actions and behavior is meaningful, too. My brother-in-law saw a need, worked to meet that need for his sons and daughter, and then took the responsibility to return the apartment to its original condition before they left. The example of those attributes has served his children well since that experience. They are interesting, creative, and responsible as they are becoming the adults God intended them to be.

# A Place for All Dads: Relationships

*Fatherhood is pretending the present*
*you love most is soap-on-a-rope.*
Bill Cosby

# IF IT AIN'T BROKE, DON'T BREAK IT

PAUL MUCKLEY

*Why do we profane the covenant of our ancestors*
*by being unfaithful to one another? . . .*
*So be on your guard, and do not be*
*unfaithful to the wife of your youth.*
MALACHI 2:10, 15 NIV

I have a philosophy: Things are never as good fixed as they were before you broke them.

Like any good father, I've shared my philosophy with my kids. Over and over. And over and over again. And over and. . .well, you know.

But the trail of battered and broken toys throughout our house provides evidence that my philosophy has yet to sink in. What may be sinking in, I'm afraid, is my forehead—from the way I slap it as the latest toy casualties arrive in my lap.

Even a Neanderthal dad, though, will do his best to repair his kids' beloved playthings, using whatever combination of tools, fasteners, and good old American ingenuity he can muster.

Kids think it's easy. In fact, my kids believe Scotch tape will fix anything. Wheel came off your Tonka truck? Put some tape on it. Notched the edge of your Wii disk? Bring out the tape. Broke some branches off the shrubbery because you were running through the mulch bed? Tape will fix it!

On occasion, even I'll use tape, though I prefer the heavy-duty stuff. There was the time I designed a fashionable duct tape turtleneck for California Blaine, Barbie's surfer-dude "friend." (If I were Barbie's beau, Ken, I'd watch out for that guy. . .he seems the type to smooth talk an all-American girl into a Barbie Harley ride into the sunset.)

Maybe I judge Blaine too harshly. Perhaps he knows his life will be short, and he's just trying to grab all the gusto he can. It seems Blaine's injection-molded family line has passed down a genetic defect, a problem with his neck that causes his head to—how can we say this delicately?—fall off.

Sadly for Blaine, my daughter quickly discovered this weakness and made his head—how shall I say this delicately?—fall off. Dr. Dad was immediately paged to the surgery suite for an emergency reattachment.

I pulled out a tube of high-tech, space-age glue that warns, if misused, might stick your fingers together until Jesus comes back. For some strange reason, though, it doesn't seem to bind plastic. Blaine's head kept—there's just no way to say this delicately—falling off. Hence the duct tape turtleneck, and lots of snarky whispers on the Barbie party circuit.

You know, it's always better to preserve what you have than to try and fix it after it breaks. That's especially true of relationships—the connection you share with your kids, the bond you have with your wife. The prophet Malachi reports God's own warning: Guard your spirit. Don't lose your heart.

Nor, I might add, your head.

# Can Anyone Say, "Amen"?

P. Reginald Legume

*Let us consider one another in order to stir up love and good works, not forsaking the assembling of ourselves together, as is the manner of some.*

Hebrews 10:24–25 NKJV

Church.

Scary, isn't it?

Enough said? Perhaps.

But, at the moment, I still have four hundred seventy-two words to go. So like my mom used to say, "If you can't say something nice about someone, just say the first thing that pops into your head." No, my mom never said that—in public. What she said was, "If you can't say something nice about someone, *don't say anything at all.*"

Oh well, sorry, Mom!

If you're a Christian, you've probably been to church. But, like myself—a seasoned, mature believer—after going to church for a while, you just might find yourself asking some "tough" questions. Questions like: *"Why in the world do I keep coming back?"*

Thankfully, the Bible has a simple, step-by-step plan to make churchgoing fun. Let's take a look at how it works:

## Step 1.
*Let us not give up meeting together,
as some are in the habit of doing.*

Sheesh! God thinks of everything, doesn't He? Why would God tell us not to give up meeting together? Because He knew that once we got around each other for five minutes, *giving up meeting together is exactly what we'd want to do!*

What could *possibly* cause such an immature, unreasonable reaction, you ask? Well, consider this: After *three solid hours* of modern worship[1] followed by *three more hours*[2] of preaching and teaching, we long for the moment when the pastor finally says, "Amen!"[3] and we can slither out of our pew and sneak down the back stairs into the parking lot before anyone can ask us if we'd like to give up our vacation to the Outer Banks to teach Vacation Bible School.

Which leads us to. . .

## Step 2.
*Let us encourage one another—
and all the more as you see the Day approaching.*

---

1. Like Woodstock, but louder and with more guitars.
2. Okay, twenty-five minutes.
3. "Who wants to go to Cracker Barrel?"

I know just what you're thinking. All things considered, we should probably encourage one another to go out for a round of golf instead. As you see *"The Day"*[4] approaching—cue the theme music from *Jaws*—it's good to consider one important point.

With this cornucopia of blessings awaiting you each and every Sunday for the rest of your earthly life, *why wouldn't you* want to roll out of bed and head off to church?

It's simple! God has a *perfectly good reason* for wanting you to assemble yourself together.

What reason, you ask? It's the exact same reason *you* use on *your* kids when *they* don't want to do something you told them to do: *"Because I said so!"*

As you only want what's best for your kids, God wants what's best for you (His kid)—even if you can't see what exactly is "best" in the present moment. So keep on meeting with other believers, and see how your life is blessed because of it. Can I get an "amen"?

---

4. You know what I'm talking about.

# A Place for
Everything. . .

Paul Muckley

*We have different gifts, according to the grace
given to each of us. If your gift is prophesying,
then prophesy in accordance with your faith; if it
is serving, then serve; if it is teaching, then teach;
if it is to encourage, then give encouragement;
if it is giving, then give generously; if it is to lead,
do it diligently; if it is to show mercy, do it cheerfully.*

Romans 12:6–8 niv

"A place for everything, and everything in its place."
Yeah, right.

Speak that nice, logical, orderly adage to my kids,
and somehow they hear "A place for everything, and
everything all over the place."

For years now, we've been working on the concept
of hanging up coats. No, son, you do not "hang up"
your coat in the middle of the living room floor. And
why, oh why, does the TV remote wander away from
the entertainment center? There's no earthly reason for

it to be found in our unfinished basement.

One of my favorite phrases (well, maybe not "favorite" but certainly "most often used") is "That's not where that goes!" The aquarium net doesn't belong in the litter box. . .the string trimmer cord doesn't go on your fishing rod. . .the business end of the flyswatter shouldn't be anywhere near anything that might at any time touch anybody's lips.

Dads worth their salt (perhaps smelling salts) will say "That's not where that goes!" when one of their kids—typically a son—starts putting things into various bodily openings. There's the ever-popular bacon-bits-up-the-nose trick, and we'll never forget our Barbie-shoe-in-the-ear experience. An emergency room visit followed the latter, and—since the tiny footwear resisted all efforts at a simple extraction—the doctor had to call in a special surgical tool. (At a special surgical price, of course.)

The granddaddy of all "that's not where that goes" stories features four-year-old Mr. Barbie-Shoe-in-the-Ear sticking a plastic marble into a certain unmentionable place, the name of which happens to rhyme with "ear."

It happened in the bathtub, where he was enjoying a good soak with several favorite toys. Looking up with a proverbial Cheshire cat smile, he told his mother, "It's up there."

"What's up where?" was her response.

"It's up there," he repeated.

"What's. . .up. . .where?" she asked again, with emphasis.

Turns out, it's nothing a good dose of mineral oil can't fix.

Though everything came out well in the end (ha ha!), we still try to convince our kids that there are right and wrong, good and bad, proper and improper places for all the things they own or use. "A place for everything, and everything in its place" makes a lot of sense.

But what if we personalized the saying to "a place for every*one*, and everyone in his place"? Then you might be talking about spiritual gifts and how we use them. God gives all His sons (daughters, too) some special interest or ability, all designed to serve others in the family. Every guy has a place of service, where he ought to be serving.

So what are your gifts? Where should you be serving? If you don't know, why not talk to your pastor and try to figure things out?

Right after you hang up your coat.

# EASIER TO BE A PHILISTINE

P. REGINALD LEGUME

*"A new command I give you: Love one another.*
*As I have loved you, so you must love one another."*
JOHN 13:34 NIV

"Still water runs deep."

That's one of those classic sayings filled with meaning and significance that needs to be repeated over and over again. The phrase "still water runs deep" is an idiom[1] dreamed up a long time ago, in a galaxy far, far away, on a planet that—unlike our own—*was not* filled with people who are *completely out of their ever-loving minds.*

Have you been going crazy lately? I know I have. We live in a crazy world—a crazy world filled with *crazy* people. And to top it all off, we have to *love* these crazy people—to which I say, "AAAARRRRGGGGHHHH!" Yes, that is very possibly the *craziest* thing of all.

Have you ever tried to love a crazy person? Not so easy, is it?

The stuff Jesus says sounds simple enough at first.

---

1. You know they're out there.

"Love your neighbor." Anyone can do that, right? Well just try it then, Mr. Smarty-Pants! Take last weekend, for example. Last Friday night our new neighbors decided to invite a few hundred thousand of their frat-house buddies (who obviously had just tunneled their way out of Alcatraz) over for a time of fun and "fellowship."

Now, I love the spirited high jinks of a group of enthusiastic young people as much as the next guy. And there's nothing more idyllic than a beautiful, green suburban front yard parked to capacity with colorful pickup trucks filled with even more colorful people who are saying and doing colorful things all over your front yard and driveway that I cannot mention here, because if I do my editor will delete them.[2]

So what's the big deal? Why am I so sensitive? So the neighbors had a little party. Know what? You're probably right. I'm being unreasonable. After all, I have a lot of great neighbors who have parties all the time.

But once the old clock-on-the-wall began to tick past two-thirty in the morning, festivities raging on at a volume just below the average Steelers/Browns play-off game, our bedroom filling with the dreamy, summertime aroma of Tiki-Torch smoke, my charitable Christian heart began to fill up with certain, I shall refer to them here as, "uncharitable thoughts."

Thoughts like the lyrics to the Mr. Rogers song "It's You I Like" you ask? Not exactly, but you're close.

---

2. This paragraph has been deleted for your protection—the Editors.

I seriously started thinking. . .*Saul killed his thousands. David killed his tens-of-thousands!*

Let's face it—it's easier to be a Philistine. No rules. No morals. No boundaries. No Bible. *No nothing!* Crazy? Yes. But those are the people Jesus wants us to love.

Looks like I still have a bit of work to do on that one.

But hey, I just found out that *my other new neighbor* adopted a pit bull (no kidding!). So, yes, at least things are finally beginning to look up.

# USING SOMEONE ELSE'S GIFTS

GAYLE LINTZ

*There are different kinds of gifts,*
*but the same Spirit distributes them.*
*There are different kinds of service, but the same Lord.*
*There are different kinds of working, but in all*
*of them and in everyone it is the same God at work.*
1 CORINTHIANS 12:4–6 NIV

I was in high school when my dad started jogging. He bought some blue running shoes and running clothes. Also, he bought a little night-light for the kitchen, to help him get easily through the house in the early morning darkness, on his way out to jog. He switched it on each evening at bedtime, and switched it off after his early morning run. It worked for many, many months.

He was befuddled when it quit working. He unplugged it, removed the bulb, and got out his tools. He worked and worked, trying to figure out the problem and repair it. No luck. He took it completely apart and finally just threw out all the pieces. Mother liked the look of the old one, so they bought another one just like it. At home, they plugged it in, and we all admired the soft glow. Dad said he hoped this little fixture would last longer than the previous one. Then someone remarked that, wouldn't it be funny if the problem wasn't the fixture but. . .

"I kept that other bulb," Dad said. He retrieved the old bulb and put it into the new night-light. Plugged it in; switched it on. Nothing. He looked ruefully at the trash can. Apparently, he had dismantled a perfectly good night-light just because the bulb had burned out.

Many dads are good with their hands. They can fix anything. They have great tools and know how to use them.

My dad was good with his words. In the army, he was a whiz at transmitting and receiving Morse code. In college, after the war, he seesawed between being a college English professor or becoming a lawyer. (He went with law.) He taught adult Sunday school for forty years. For ten years, also during that time, he taught children's church. He established a Toastmaster's group at his workplace and even stayed active with them for twenty years after he retired. He might not have been skilled with tools, but he was a master at writing and speaking.

I still see, daily, the example of his less-than-perfect handyman skills. I live with my family in my childhood home. In the master bedroom, often several times a day, I turn the light on and off. However, this night-light operates a bit differently. I have to push the switch down to turn the light on and push it up to turn it off (backward from a typical night-light switch). Many years ago, when the switch stopped working, at some point in the past, Dad had gotten out his tools and replaced the defective one, installing the new one upside down. It's a lasting reminder to me that nobody's an expert in everything.

God gifts us all differently. We just need to figure out what we're good at and when we need to ask for help.

# CHILLAXIN' WITH THE ULTIMATE FATHER: INNER LIFE

*The qualities of a great man are vision, integrity, courage, understanding, the power of articulation, and profundity of character.*

DWIGHT EISENHOWER

# My Thumb-Sucking Theology

## Paul M. Miller

*Where can I go from your Spirit? Where can I flee from*
*your presence? If I go up to the heavens, you are there;*
*if I make my bed in the depths, you are there.*

Psalm 139:7–8 NIV

A thumb-sucking son can be most disconcerting for a
dad who has huge expectations for his kid. Thumb-
suckers don't seem to equate with world-shakers, or even
people-movers.

In Tim's case, it all started when he was a preschooler.
In the beginning it was an innocent activity that he
engaged in when he was tired. Evidently he found
security in his cute stubby little finger.

At first I thought it was better than those plastic
devices that can be seen protruding out of kids' mouths,
and I'm sure it's more manly than dragging around one
of the blankets that Linus of *Peanuts* fame carries.

When Tim started kindergarten, he was still addicted
to his thumb. His pediatrician laughed at my concern

and asked, "Who are you more concerned about—Tim or your reputation?"

Then it was time for first-grade, and I must admit, neither his thumb nor his teeth had yet become deformed. But my ego continued to give me problems.

Our next-door neighbor laughed when I confessed my chagrin to him. "Just be glad he doesn't stick his index finger into his nose while he's sucking. My kid did that!"

One Sunday after lunch I decided to have a man-to-man chat with my son. No, birds and bees had nothing to do with it, but the first digit on his left hand did. (Tim always kept his right hand available for holding ice cream bars and other treats.)

The trump card of that Sunday afternoon conversation was, "God doesn't like it when He sees you sucking your thumb." This made the issue no longer a Dad-thing, but it was now a God-thing.

Two days later, on a trip down into the basement, I found Tim sitting by the furnace with his thumb between his lips reading a book.

"Tim, what in the world. . . ?"

Removing his chubby finger, he replied, "Daddy, I have it all figured out. Remember you said God doesn't like to see me sucking my thumb?"

"Yes, I remember."

"Well, if I suck my thumb down here, God can't see me."

"What do you mean, 'God can't see me'?"

"Just that. There's the roof, the ceiling in my bedroom [on the second floor], my floor, the ceiling above the living room [on the first floor], the living room floor, and then the ceiling here in the basement. I bet God can't see through all that!"

Years later, when Tim had graduated from college—having never worn braces nor had thumb repair surgery, I asked, "How did you finally break the habit?"

"I guess I just woke up one morning and decided I had all the security anyone needed. Our home was always a secure place."

With great relief I asked, "And who was the center of our family security?"

Tim smiled and replied, "Yeah, I know, you want to hear me give you all the credit for our family security."

"Well. . . ," I blustered. Then he gave his one-word answer.

"God."

# WHERE ARE YOU?

CONOVER SWOFFORD

*Then the LORD God called to Adam and said to him,*
*"Where are you?"*
GENESIS 3:9 NKJV

Stephen was frantically searching for his three-year-old son, Jack. He called for him over and over, but there was no answer. Finally, Stephen went to the back door and called, "Jack, are you in the woods?"

"Yes," came the answer.

"You know you aren't allowed in the woods," Stephen said. "You come here right now."

"No," said the little voice.

"What do you mean no?" Stephen demanded. "Come here right now."

"I can't," Jack replied.

"What do you mean you can't?" Stephen asked anxiously. "Are you hurt?"

"No," Jack called, "but if I come in, you will spank me."

Everybody may not need a spanking, but we all need discipline. Our children know when someone needs correcting—usually someone other than themselves. People may argue over the type of discipline a child should receive, but they agree that children should be disciplined.

A father took his three-year-old son to a child psychologist who told him that he was being too negative and should not say the word "no" to his son.

"Oh really?" said the man. "So if he runs out into traffic, I should just let him go?"

The psychologist had no answer for him.

The Bible says that whom the Lord loves, He chastens (Hebrews 12:6). Just like God disciplines us to keep our souls safe for eternity, we discipline our children to keep them physically safe on this earth and spiritually safe for eternity. Proverbs says that we will save them from death by correcting them (Proverbs 23:14). We may literally save them from death here by not allowing them to do dangerous things.

Spiritual discipline is different than physical discipline. Spiritual discipline helps protect the souls of our children. When our children understand the importance of spiritual discipline (and when they practice spiritual disciplines), we are helping to protect them from spiritual death. One of the best ways to do this is to teach our children to hide God's Word in their heart. We need to teach them to memorize verses that will instruct them in the way God wants them to go. God entrusted our children to us. We need to entrust them back to Him.

Discipline often implies fear. However, fear of the Lord doesn't mean being afraid of Him or being afraid that He will punish us. Fear of the Lord means being careful not to do anything that would grieve Him. But if we have done something wrong, we can go boldly to Him, confess our wrongdoing, and know that He will forgive us and not remember our sin any more.

God created us in His image and likeness. He has placed His Spirit within us. We don't have to be afraid of what He will do to us. Instead we can take comfort in the fact that no matter what we do, God loves us unconditionally.

# ALL IN THE FAMILY

PAUL MUCKLEY

*He determines the number of the stars and calls them*
*each by name. Great is our Lord and mighty in power;*
*his understanding has no limit.*

PSALM 147:4–5 NIV

Collectors build their collections in various ways.
If you're into old cars or firearms, you might frequent swap meets. If you like postage stamps, you could go the mail-order route. If you enjoy interesting rocks, you could just snatch up pretty specimens when you happen across them.

None of these options are recommended for acquiring children.

When it comes to building a family, there are really only two methods: Have the children yourself (well, let your wife have them) or adopt. My wife and I did the latter.

Benefits of adoption: Mom doesn't worry about that weight gain/labor pain/stretch marks stuff. . .Dad doesn't worry about Mom worrying over those things. . .

neither worries about the kid getting Dad's hawk nose or receding hairline or Mom's. . .well, Mom wouldn't have any physical traits to beware of, would she?

Drawbacks? Really, they're not that different than having babies the old-fashioned way. There are up-front, middle-front, and back-front costs (you're in it for at least eighteen years, buddy), and there are no guarantees of just how it will work out. But if you can guarantee just how your *own* flesh and blood will turn out, you probably have a multimillion-copy bestseller on your hands.

One major difference with adoption is the time frame—usually, you'll have considerably less than nine months to prepare. Our oldest child arrived about a week and a half after we first learned of her, and we often joked about our "nine-day pregnancy."

But that was an eternity compared to our third child. With our daughter at seven, our son at five, and ourselves at, *ahem,* forty-something, adopting again was the last thing on our minds. God, however, unveiled His plan—and perhaps that legendary sense of humor—by giving us a twenty-four hour notice on our last (we hope!) adoption.

The baby and our daughter had the same birth mother, who called our adoption agency asking if we would take this child, too. How do you say no to that?

So the next morning, on the ninety-minute drive to pick up the kid, we realized that in the rush of events we hadn't even considered a name. Somehow, just calling him "Number 3" seemed wrong—though that would be considerably less embarrassing to a kid than calling him "Number 1" or "Number 2."

We'd named our daughter after a rock-and-roll song, but since boys' monikers are somewhat rarer in the genre, we turned to the bands themselves—and stumbled across one of our favorites: *Journey*. It was a cool idea, reflective of our new life ahead. . .but ultimately seemed a little "hippie" for us.

In the end, we went with a not-overly-common-yet-kind-of-cool Scottish name, one that confuses almost everyone who hears it. Oh well.

Thankfully, God "gets" Niall's name, just as He knows and understands all of ours. If He calls every star in the universe by name, then God certainly knows each and every one of us.

And He loves when we call *Him* "Dad."

# THE ROAD TO EURO DISNEY

## DAVID MCLAUGHLAN

*"I will lead the blind by ways they have not known,*
*along unfamiliar paths I will guide them;*
*I will turn the darkness into light before them*
*and make the rough places smooth.*
*These are the things I will do; I will not forsake them."*

ISAIAH 42:16 NIV

This was supposed to be the holiday the kids would never forget—and, so far, they haven't! We were heading for Euro Disney, also known as Disneyland Paris. And I had organized it!

I have to admit, I was feeling pretty pleased with my organizational abilities. The airport pickup went well, the flight was a pleasure, and it was easy enough getting onto the French railroad system from the airport.

I say easy, but with three children all under ten and all their luggage, well. . .I got distracted.

At the station there was a choice of trains leaving from the same platform. They all went along the same line, but some turned off and went to Euro Disney, others went on into Paris. And, of course, I herded the family onto the wrong train.

I clued in to my mistake when we passed the Euro Disney turnoff. We all got off at the next station and caught the next train back to our start point. All in all it added twenty minutes to the journey.

What I didn't understand was that my children had reached the developmental stage where they were beginning to grapple with the idea that their parents weren't perfect—and here I was giving them proof. "Dad took us on the wrong train!"

One of them is in the army now, another is about to be married, and the third is starting college. They have difficulty remembering anything about that trip, even though it was a big success. Every time the family gets together and starts reminiscing, the memory of that trip comes up. Less than thirty seconds later (and I have timed it) one of them will say, "Oh, that was the time Dad took us on the wrong train!"

Everything right I did on that trip is consigned to the wastebin of their memories. I am convinced my momentary mistake, will *never* be forgotten. I've even started mentioning it myself just to get the mockery over and done with!

What's the lesson from all of this?

As much as we'd like to think that we're quick to forget other's sins, we aren't. We love remembering our hurts. We enjoy making friends uncomfortable, reminding them of their mistakes. And we often take joy in recalling uncomfortable moments when others have messed up.

I'm thankful that God is not like this. Despite our mistakes, He does not forsake us. No matter how bad our planning and how rotten the results of our own hands, God never reminds us of our wrong turns.

# WE REALLY BELONG TO EACH OTHER

PAUL M. MILLER

*Therefore each of you must put off falsehood
and speak truthfully to your neighbor,
for we are all members of one body.*
EPHESIANS 4:25 NIV

Family solidarity can best be tested on a family vacation traveled over too many miles in an automobile.

Most of us fathers can recall the times our travel-jangled nerves have caused us to pull the family car to a halt on the shoulder of the road and declare with patriarchal authority, "If you kids don't stop arguing. . ."

"But Daddy, Tim came over to my half of the seat."

"I don't care what he did, Lisa. If you don't. . ."

Yeah, I sure remember those days; stopping at a roadside picnic table at noon. . .Lisa's predictable, "Aren't we there yet?". . .devotions in a motel room before starting out in the morning.

On one such morning, it was Tim's turn to read. He selected the fourth chapter of Ephesians and read from his *Bible*: "So you must stop telling lies. Tell each other the truth, because we all belong to each other in the same body" (4:25 NCV).

There was silence from both Tim and Lisa as we repacked the car. We were well on our way then Lisa blurted out, "Tim, were you calling me a liar back there?"

"If the shoe fits, wear it!"

"What shoe?"

To change the subject, Tim asked, "Remember when Lisa was learning which shoe went on which foot?" We all recalled, at Lisa's expense, the morning she put her shoes on by herself, and how her mom noticed the right shoe was on the left foot.

That's when she said, "Honey, your shoes are on the wrong feet."

And that's when Lisa said, "But Mommy, I know they're my feet."

Even Lisa had to smile, though not remembering the occasion. Then she observed, "I must have been a cute baby," causing Tim to feign a coughing fit.

All was quiet for a few miles until I returned to our original topic of the morning—the meaning of the scripture Tim had read back in the motel, causing Lisa to look uncomfortable.

What was meant by, "We all belong to each other"?

There was more silence, then Tim spoke. "We really do belong to each other, don't we?"

"And we belong to Jesus, too," added a more thoughtful Lisa.

I won't say the imaginary dividing line across the backseat of our old Chevy was never drawn again. Nor will I pretend that we heard our last sibling argument from that day on. But I will readily testify that at least the four in our Chevy Impala had a new understanding of our relationship to each other—and to Jesus Christ.

# HOW MANY BADS MAKE A GOOD?

## DAVID MCLAUGHLAN

*"He himself bore our sins" in his body on the cross,*
*so that we might die to sins and live for righteousness;*
*"by his wounds you have been healed."*

1 PETER 2:24 NIV

Aaarrrggghhh! It was one of those mornings.

I had been tasked with seeing the boys off to school. As I put out food for our collie, a scream from the living room pierced the walls. Dropping the food on the floor (for our obliging dog to lap up) I rushed to the living room expecting puddles of blood.

I looked in horror as Mark (eight) had put both feet against the back of Kyle (six) and heaved him off the couch. Kyle had banged his arm on the coffee table mid-flight, hence the screams.

Why had Mark done that? Well, because Kyle had bitten Mark's thigh. Why had Kyle bitten Mark's thigh? Because Mark had been sitting on Kyle's face. An argument ensued. Each time I told one of them how ridiculous they were acting, their instant response was to say the other brother had done something worse first.

Letting go of my first response (which was to shove little bits of the dog food up their noses), I tried reasoning. "Just because another person does a bad thing does not give you the right to do a bad thing. If he's wrong in what he does," I said, pointing emphatically at my younger son, "then doing wrong in return does not make you right. Two wrongs don't make a right!"

I checked to see if either of them needed an ambulance, and returned to see if the dog had finished cleaning the floor for me.

A couple of minutes later I heard raised voices from the living room, but before I could return I heard Mark take control. "If you do that, we'll just get into trouble again," he said. Kyle's reply was muffled, and I couldn't quite make it out. But Mark's tone, when he replied, sounded a lot like mine.

I came close to bursting back into the room, but I stopped when Mark's words filled the doorway.

"That doesn't matter, Kyle," he said. "Remember, two bads don't make a wrong!"

I nearly burst out laughing. Wrong words, right idea!

Then I thought about it. Maybe he wasn't the only one to use the wrong words. "Two wrongs don't make a right." It was an expression I had heard all my life. I knew what it meant, but had I ever thought it through?

Just as no amount of bad behavior would make me stop loving Mark and Kyle, so no amount of sin would ever separate me from Jesus. If, by some miracle, I lived a life with only two sins, or bads, He would make them a good. If I brought three bads to Him, or four, or five, or the astronomical number I am bound to have committed—He will, through the best possible kind of Fatherly love, make them ALL a good!

# It Hurts Me More

James Low

*We considered him punished by God,*
*stricken by him, and afflicted.*
*But he was pierced for our transgressions,*
*he was crushed for our iniquities;*
*the punishment that brought us peace was on him,*
*and by his wounds we are healed.*

Isaiah 53:4–5 NIV

As soon as I did it, I knew I was in trouble.

The multitude of times my parents told me to stop didn't deter me from having to learn the hard way. I earned myself a spanking. Before you object to my having been spanked, let me clarify. I was of a certain age where I knew full well the consequences of my actions, and that spanking was a "last resort" by which my parents lovingly disciplined me. I also knew that it was often the only deterrent that kept my rather rebellious side at bay during my "colorful" childhood.

What I remember about being spanked was that the actual spanking wasn't the problem. No, it was more the anticipation of the event that was agonizing. This was especially true as I waited in my room for my dad to come and administer the punishment. The thing that puzzled me about being spanked, however, was that when my dad actually spanked me, he would first come down to my level and look me in the eyes, and say, "This hurts me more than it hurts you."

I remember thinking "What?" Even then I knew the obvious solution would be to call the whole thing off so as to avoid hurting my dad (not to mention my tush). I didn't understand. It wasn't until my wife and I contemplated how we would discipline our children that I started to understand and realize how true my father's words were. Not only did I realize the pain that grieves a father's heart in having to discipline his children, but also reflecting on my relationship with my heavenly Father, I realized how perfectly these words suited the Christian's condition.

Before I came to know the Lord as Savior, I had to come to terms with the fact that I was a sinner. I danced around this under the pretense of being "a good person" for a long time, but there was no way around it. I was a sinner, and my sin demanded punishment before God. I was in trouble. I can tell you that the anticipation of awaiting punishment from the heavenly Father was far more agonizing than anything I encountered before.

The Lord arrived, and unable to avoid Him I turned to face Him. Once I did, I knew it was true—dealing with my sin hurt Him more than it hurt me. God came down to my level, looked my sin full in the face, and paid the punishment for my sinfulness by way of His Son Jesus Christ who suffered an agonizing death on the cross. From then on, I was His child.

It is this monumental grace, by which we are saved, that we are called as fathers to extend to and instill in our children. It doesn't overlook the need for punishment, but it is rooted in grace and gives life. Indeed it is by this grace that we love our children as our heavenly Father loves us.

# THE DAD POWERHOUSE 1: GOD'S RESCUE

*The greatness of Man's power
is the measure of his surrender.
It is not a question of who you are,
or of what you are, but whether God controls you.*
HENRIETTA C. MEARS

# ANNOYING QUESTIONS

GLENN A. HASCALL

*Hear my voice when I call, LORD;*
*be merciful to me and answer me.*
PSALM 27:7 NIV

Guess what?"

Do our children utter two words that are more distressing? Sure there's the incessant question, "Why?", and those careless behaviors associated with potty training and other forms of embarrassing social etiquette.

There are lots of annoying habits kids pick up. Where do they learn them?

"Hey Dad, guess what?" My son paused for dramatic effect. Because I didn't respond immediately he increased the level of his vocal amplification, "Guess what, Dad?"

I'm not deaf, and he really wants an answer. However, he could be talking about an event on the playground, a bug he found on a tree, or it's even possible he just had a thought he'll forget before he can actually tell me. I honestly have no clue—and there's no good answer.

"Guess what?"

"I wish I knew."

A few years ago I came up with an answer that seemed to curb my son's enthusiasm for asking this question. When he asks, I reply, "Dogs are big, cows are smelly, and frogs are green."

That's been my answer every time he utters those two words.

If he's got something to tell me, he should just tell me. I'm not a mind reader.

I am a broken man listening to a broken record asking me to guess something I am clearly incapable of presuming. I am humbled at my personal ineptitude. I often hear those two words mocking me in my sleep.

It took awhile, but the habit is nearly broken. Now if he wants to tell me something, he usually just tells me. There are very few "Guess what?" moments these days.

Imagine my surprise when I discovered I do the same thing to God. I can pray to Him using the same phrases, the same questions, the same excuses, and the same tone. Does He ever get tired of hearing me say, "I'm sorry"? Does He ever turn a deaf ear to me when I say, "Make Yourself real to my children"? Is it possible I annoy Him?

There are two children who call me dad, but how many millions call on God as their Father? How many annoying traits does He hear every day?

In the space of twenty-four hours He listens to children who fall asleep in the middle of their prayers. He hears the struggle of issues that haven't changed much over the years. He responds to hearts that start talking and forget what they were going to say—or they are so distressed they just can't come up with the right words.

"Guess what?"

He listens—He understands.

Yeah, I do feel foolish. My son is growing up, and I miss the childlike enthusiasm that showed he simply wanted to share a special moment with me. I lament the notion that I could so callously step on his enthusiasm by calling into question the way he chose to share his heart.

There is a perfect dad who resides in my heart, and I'm asking Him to continue the lifelong work of making me more like Him.

"Hey son, guess what?"

God continues the hard work of transforming me. Thanks, God, for Your patience.

# OUR KING OF THE JUNGLE

PAUL M. MILLER

*"I am the LORD your God who takes hold of your right*
*hand and says to you, Do not fear; I will help you.*
*Do not be afraid. . .for I myself will help you."*

ISAIAH 41:13–14 NIV

"Guess what kids?" I, father of two, asked my son and daughter one Friday evening. "We're going to take a super great trip this summer!"

Daughter Lisa brightened and screamed, "Disney World!" while son Tim lifted his eyes from a tropical fish book and mused, "The Great Barrier Reef?"

"Nope. Lisa you are way off. But Tim. . ."

Tim's eyes brightened. " 'But' what, Dad?" he fired back.

The kids' mom interrupted. "Dad has been asked to teach a creative writing class at our church's college in Santa Cruz, Trinidad."

I could tell that they recognized the location.

"Check the index in your book, Tim. I guarantee you'll find the Caribbean country Trinidad and Tobago."

Sure enough, there it was: three pages of magnificent color pictures showing the tropical fish that inhabit the warm waters of that southern Caribbean two-island country off the coast of Venezuela.

In two months the family was bidding good-bye to our Kansas City neighborhood, and "Hello!" to Piarco International airport just outside Port-of-Spain, Trinidad.

On a teaching day off, fellow teachers and some students took my family and me for a hike across Saddleback Trail for a picnic on the beach.

The trail to our site took us over an easy mountain range. One side of the well-worn path dropped off into a deep canyon, whose depth we really could not estimate.

The semi-jungle flora around us apparently brought the Tarzan out in Tim. All along the hike our normally quiet son shocked the group with heart-stopping King of the Jungle yells.

These Tarzan antics were good for a laugh, until he spied a thick vine draping down from one of the trees. That's when our blood ran cold.

With a whoop and jungle yell, Tim grabbed the vine and with complete ease swung out over the bottomless canyon below. His mother gasped, students applauded, sister Lisa screamed, and I couldn't wait to start the lecture about appropriate behavior.

I watched my son's adolescent glee turn into utter horror, almost as if it were happening in slow motion. It dawned on him (way too late) that nothing was keeping the vine from separating from the tree, potentially dropping him who-knows-how-far below into who-knows-what.

Later, when he was finally seated on the palm-shaded beach, I asked my shaken son, "What were you thinking?"

He answered with a question, "You mean when I was in the air, or when I landed back on the trail?"

"Don't be funny," I retorted.

"Out there in midair I remembered a Bible verse you taught me: 'I. . .will help you' [Isaiah 41:14]. I decided this was my chance to test that promise."

Later, after stern reprimands and the threat of sending him home, Tim admitted he wasn't cut out to be the King of the Apes.

On a long-distance phone call from adult Tim the other day, my son reminded me of his Caribbean escapade. After a good laugh I asked him, "Still remember your Bible verse for that day?"

"I sure do, Dad: 'I. . .will help you.' And He really has."

# STEP RELOCATION

GLENN A. HASCALL

*Your word is a lamp for my feet,
a light on my path.*
PSALM 119:105 NIV

I come from a long line of jack-of-all-trade types. My grandpa was a rancher, engineer, stagecoach driver, and police officer. He was raised in a sod house and often wore the expression of a well-aged prune dipped in lemon juice. He tried to let on that he was as crusty as over-baked bread, but we weren't fooled.

My dad could overhaul an engine, restore a '64 Mustang, cook a meaningful breakfast, and plot a garden with the comfort level of marshmallow in s'mores. His skills extended to explorer, musician, and storyteller. He's also one of the most giving men I've ever known. His facial expressions have never resembled either fruit or baked goods.

There were times Dad invited me to join him on his adventures, which made perfect sense. As his son, I felt a powerful obligation to know how to use a refurbished

1960's vehicle to dig up a garden while consuming traditional camp food.

I would take mental notes as I watched him haggle for the best price on an automobile. I climbed ladders and catwalks helping him paint dozens of homes. I leased equipment from him to start a lawn care business. We talked a lot and laughed even more. I love my dad.

Before he retired, Dad was also a closet inventor. This led to a device known as the Jociciser: a handy exercise apparatus made from a T-shaped stick and a wheelbarrow wheel. It was genius as far as eye-hand coordination was concerned, but it didn't quite catch on. There were other nearly successful ideas.

"Hey Dad," I said, as I brought my young bride to the backyard one day in summer. "What's for supper?"

He opened up the grill, and I inhaled the answer. That's when I noticed something unusual, "Did you get new lava rocks for the bottom of the grill? They look peculiar."

"I had some leftover cement, so I figured I could make my own." The response didn't surprise me. Dad has always been a genius at making things work. "I could make you a set." As we walked away, a series of explosions pounded the inside of the grill.

Dad shut off the propane, assessed the damage, smiled, and uttered something I'm certain Thomas Edison wouldn't appreciate. "Well, that didn't work" he commented in a discouraged tone. Apparently the heat from the fire made the concrete unstable and the cement bricks literally exploded, sending shards of concrete deep into our supper.

Hand injuries are also common with my dad. He uses his hands to fix things so often that it's not unusual for a few slips of the tool to require payment in skin and an impromptu attempt at freestyle yodeling.

Dad has faced his own share of difficulties in life, but complaints are uncommon. Setbacks just give him a better vantage point to work from.

God never promised that we'd be able to see everything years in advance. He only promised enough light to show us where to walk next. We may know where we want to go, but only God can provide the light we need to know if we're going in the right direction.

# There's Little Sitting
# in Babysitting

## Paul M. Miller

*Be strong in the Lord and in his great power.*
*Put on the full armor of God so that you*
*can fight against the devil's evil tricks.*
### Ephesians 6:10–11 NCV

At what point in a teen girl's babysitting career should the title be changed to "child chasing"?

My daughter Lisa found herself asking that question early in her professional life—especially when she sat the Paddock boys.

"There wasn't much sitting involved," she laughs today. "They could invent the most creative mayhem."

Lisa's school had offered a class in babysitting, and she learned the techniques of disposing, wiping, powdering, folding, applying, and pinning, none of which applied to the Paddock brothers—Troy, Craig, and Brian. ("Our little gentlemen," she'd call them.)

" 'Little gentlemen. . .' " Lisa mumbled. "Those boys are more like little terrorists. I betcha when their mom announces, 'Lisa's coming over tomorrow night,' the kids start hatching their nefarious deeds."

Worse came to worse on a Thursday afternoon when the phone rang and her mother called, "It's for you, Lisa." Then with a hand over the receiver she announced, "It's Mrs. Paddock."

"Tell her I'm sick with typhoid fever."

"Lisa!"

"Tell her I've. . ."

"Lisa!"

"Oh all right. Hello, Mrs. Paddock? This is Lisa. Sure, I'd love to sit for you tomorrow night." (If you were standing behind her, you'd have seen Lisa's crossing fingers.) "Five o'clock will be fine."

Now, here's where ol' Dad enters the narrative. . . . As always, I drive my enterprising daughter over to the Paddocks' and wait to watch her make her way to the front door, where she is greeted by a gracious Mrs. Paddock. As Lisa enters the house, she pleadingly looks back at me in near fear. Of course, my instinct is to stage some kind of rescue caper to protect her from the awaiting gang of three.

Fast-forward a couple of hours. The phone rings and a frantic, but familiar, voice pleads, "Dad, hurry, please get over here quickly. Brian [the youngest] is stuck in the laundry chute."

Sure enough, when Lisa pulls me into the house, I can hear a boy's weak voice calling out, "Help!"

Ignoring Brian's plea, I sternly ask my tearful

daughter why Brian was in the laundry chute in the first place. Her answer was pretty straightforward, "All three of them like to slide down it, but no one's gotten stuck before."

"Brian, where are your arms?" I shout up the exit opening.

"They're hooked on to my shoulders."

Ignoring his obvious answer, I continue, "Can you move your hands to above your head?"

"No. They're holding onto my basketball."

"Well, for goodness' sake, drop the ball!"

In a moment or two, a ball comes rolling out of the chute, followed by a pair of feet and pajama-clad legs, then all of Brian slid out onto the laundry room floor.

The next morning at breakfast, Lisa remembered a wise admonition from her babysitting instructor: "Always expect the unexpected."

Right on! Truer words have never been spoken for babysitting or fathering: "Be strong. . . . Put on the full armor of God. . . ."

# THOU SHALT NOT KILL

P. REGINALD LEGUME

*Christ loved the church and gave himself for it.*
EPHESIANS 5:25 NCV

God has a sense of humor. Don't you think so? Consider this: My family and I are involved in a church plant. Yes, I know—I hear your tender words flowing like living water from deep inside a heart of Christian love: *"ARE YOU ABSOLUTELY CRAZY?"*

Why on earth would my family want to leave the comfort and stability of an established, well-run, thriving, Bible teaching, worshipping church that looks after its flock and reaches out to others?

Gluttons for punishment, I guess.

If you've ever been involved in a church plant, you know it can be challenging to say the least. If you haven't, but are considering it, I have these words of advice: *Run for the hills!*[1]

My family and I are currently in the fifth year of our one-year church-plant commitment. Needless to say, most of the other folks who volunteered are either back behind bars, or are currently attending the Church

---

1. Or, alternately, *"ARE YOU ABSOLUTELY CRAZY?"*

of the Padded Cell with complimentary straitjacket service. This experience has truly opened my eyes, and in response to what those eyes have seen I humbly say, *"Aaaaarrrrrgggggghhhhhhh!"*

I am no spring chicken. In fact, by all accounts, I am currently older than dirt. One of the most difficult challenges of this "journey" has been trying my best[2] to allow people of the younger generation—and by the younger generation I mean actual human beings who are currently about the age of my own children—to commit acts of leadership upon me repeatedly and with joy.

What's the big deal? Problems with leadership, you say? Not so fast. . .I'm on the Leadership Team!

I like people as much as the next guy. Okay, not really. Taken individually, people aren't that bad. But put a bunch of them around a conference table and you have what the Bible refers to as "The Abomination That Causes Desolation."

Just kidding!

I'm a worker bee. I don't like meetings. But meetings are a part of life,[3] and so as a responsible Christian dad I go to them. It was at a meeting like this that our young pastor asked each of us to think of one word and one scripture that summed up our experience as church leaders.

I'm not one to over-spiritualize things, but when you hear God's voice, you hear it. And what God said to me was; *"Your word: Long-suffering—your scripture: Thou shalt not kill."*[4]

---

2. Yes, your best would have been better.

3. So are taxes and poison ivy.

4. Okay, maybe I'm exaggerating—(just a bit).

Jesus loves the church. And believe it or not, I do, too. Perhaps my current road is more about character building than blessings and rest. But my family and I are walking the road Jesus set before us. Does it have a few bumps? Yes. But "We know that in all things God works for the good of those who love him, who have been called according to his purpose" (Romans 8:28 NIV).

So if you're looking for me, I'll be in church. I'm the one down in front wearing the denim straitjacket.

# FRIED CHICKEN

## CONOVER SWOFFORD

*Don't hold back training from a child.*
*If you correct him, he won't die.*
*So correct him. Then you will save him from death.*
PROVERBS 23:13–14 NIrV

One afternoon, five-year-old twins, Keane and Kiley were rough-housing. Their parents had been lecturing them for a week about the perils of this type of behavior. A few days prior, Kiley had ended up getting a tooth knocked out after Keane's head and her mouth collided.

This day their father, John, called the kids upstairs and proceeded to tell them that they were to play separately because they couldn't control themselves and were getting too wild.

Keane leaned over with his head in his hands and said, "Dad, are you thinkin' what I'm thinkin'?"

John assumed Keane would go into the whole "somebody's gonna get hurt if you keep playing like that" speech.

Before John could reply, Keane continued as serious as could be, "I'm thinkin' fried chicken!" (Imagine a heavy emphasis on the words "fried chicken.")

John could barely keep a straight face. He said "Go play!" so that Keane and Kiley would leave the room and he could laugh without the kids seeing him. He was, after all, trying to lay down the law and be the stern Dad!

Sometimes you have to wonder if kids know they're creating a diversion or if they are just naturally thinking about other things. Perhaps this happens to us when we try to pray. Instead of thinking about our communication with God, we are wondering what we're going to have for supper. Or maybe we think we can divert God's attention from something that we've done. We tend to lean on our own understanding. However, when we do that, we don't understand what the problem really is. And while we are trying to figure it out by ourselves, we aren't trusting God to solve the problem for us.

It's tempting to think that we can divert God's attention so that He doesn't see what we really need and then try and fix our problems using our own strength. Sometimes, instead of following God's clear instructions, we look for a loophole so we solve our problems on our own. But what happens when we do? . . .

Abraham is a great example for us. God promised Abraham and Sarah a son. Sarah got tired of waiting. According to the custom of that day, a barren wife could give her maidservant to her husband and any child that resulted would be considered the wife's child. But when Hagar was expecting, she became arrogant toward Sarah. Sarah became even more aware of her barrenness and, in a fit of jealousy, made Abraham send Hagar away. We know that Hagar's descendants are the Arab nation. Sarah leaned on her own understanding and started a war that lasts to this very day.

If we lean on our own understanding, often the problem only gets worse. However, if we leave it up to God, He will work everything out for good—according to His will (and there's nothing better than that). Trust Him today!

# THOSE DIFFICULT QUESTIONS

DAVID MCLAUGHLAN

*"See that you do not despise one of these little ones.
For I tell you that their angels in heaven always
see the face of my Father in heaven."*
MATTHEW 18:10 NIV

Children ask the most ridiculous questions!

Like when Stacey was doing a history project in third grade. She wanted to tell me all about it and I listened, genuinely interested. Then she said, "Dad," and got a faraway look in her eye. "What was it *really* like back then?"

The project was on the War of Independence! Wow. . . I have never felt so old! But she sincerely wanted to know, so I ignored the unintended insult and pretended like I had actually been there. The things a dad will do for his child's education.

The most vivid memory I have of one of my kids' questions came a few years before that. Stacey was five, her little sister Mandy was three. Their little beds lay parallel to each other with just enough space between them for a dad and a book.

I was the resident storyteller and, at this point, the routine went like this—I would help Mandy read from a picture book with a few easy words while Stacey, being older, read to herself. Then I would read them both a story, hoping they would fall asleep during it.

That evening, Mandy's book was about animal mommies and their babies. You know—the mommy is a cow, her baby is a calf, the mommy is a duck, her baby is a duckling, and so on.

When I finally finished the final installment of the communal story, Stacey was asleep but Mandy was still awake.

"Daaad," she said, lost in thought.

"Yes, sweetheart?"

"If the calf's mommy was the cow. . .then who was the cow's mommy? Because everybody has to have a mommy, don't they?"

Good question. So I explained how mommies had mommies and they had mommies, and the same applied to people. I bent over to give her a good-night kiss.

"Daaad."

"Yes, sweetheart?"

Where did the very first mommy come from?"

"Well. . .I guess God made the first mommy. Now, good. . ."

"Daaad?" And her attention seemed to be very far away indeed.

"Did God have a mommy?" Yikes!

"No, darling, I don't think so. And I don't know how that works, but. . ." There and then I was all too aware of my distance from God. This little one was only three years from her Creator. My reply suddenly seemed like a very real, very possible option. "Tell you what," I said softly and with respect. "Think about it for a while. And, if you figure it out. . .will you tell me? Please?"

Mandy nodded solemnly.

"I will, Dad."

I walked down the stairs a much humbler man. Only too aware of how little my education, my experience, and my position at work benefitted me when it came to the really important things. To answer those really difficult questions I needed the heart of a child.

# A DAD'S GOTTA
# BE HAPPY:
# PEACE

*A father carries pictures where his money used to be.*
AUTHOR UNKNOWN

# AFRAID OF THE. . .

PAUL MUCKLEY

*"Be strong and courageous. Do not be afraid;*
*do not be discouraged, for the LORD your God*
*will be with you wherever you go."*

JOSHUA 1:9 NIV

Kids, by nature, are scaredy-cats.

They're afraid of the dark. They're afraid of new situations. They're afraid of things that really confuse their dads. One of my kids, for example, couldn't handle *Veggie Tales* because the characters lacked arms and legs. Never mind that they *do* have eyes, noses, and talking mouths.

Dads stand as the great bulwark of protection and encouragement for frightened kids. In their eyes, dads aren't afraid of anything.

But, truth be told, even dads have their phobias. Grown-up guys fear job losses, health problems, dings on the new car, even baldness. What else explains Rogaine, Hair Club for Men, and toupee-in-a-can?

Personally, I hate moths. They don't make me scream like the proverbial girl, but I just don't like 'em. (Did you know there's a North American moth bigger than many birds? Somewhere out there, *Hyalophora cecropia* is fluttering around on six-inch wings. . .that's kind of disturbing.)

But nothing ever struck fear into my heart like the words of my preschool daughter: "Daddy, I have to go to the bathroom."

Oh, at home it wasn't so bad. But what if we were in a public place? Even worse, what if my toddler son was along, too?

Let's face it: Men's bathrooms aren't places we want to take our little girls. Guys aren't known as the most sanitary creatures on the planet, ranking in scientific studies only slightly above the common housefly.

So bathroom visits were always accompanied by a lot of "Don't touch that!" "Get off the floor!" "Don't crawl behind that toilet!"

That last order was most often directed at the male toddler. I guess while sissie is conducting her necessary business, a two-year-old needs to find some activity to fill those fifteen seconds.

I've no idea how clearly developed a toddler's thoughts are, but if I could have read the boy's mind, my guess is the story would have gone something like this:

*Gee, I'm in a room without toys. Wow, is this*
*boring. Hmm, what can I do? Say, what's this*
*funny white thing hanging on the wall? Hey,*
*I can stick my hand down in that water!*

It seems as if kids are drawn to dirty, germy bathroom surfaces like a moth is to a flame. And both images give me chills.

Fortunately, most bathrooms also feature sinks and soap—and I made sure my kids scrubbed for what seemed like hours to them. Moths—excepting, perhaps, the *Hyalophora cecropia*—can be managed with a fly-swatter. As fears go, most are small and silly.

But what about those bigger scares? Bad news from the doctor, pink slips, relationship problems? That's where God's promise to Joshua comes in: "'The Lord your God will be with you wherever you go.'"

If we can truly believe that, then the rest of Joshua 1:9 falls into place: "'Be strong and courageous. Do not be afraid; do not be discouraged.'"

Afraid of [your fear here]? Remember that God is with you.

# It's the Taking Part That Counts

## David McLaughlan

*For this reason he had to be made like them,*
*fully human in every way, in order that he might become*
*a merciful and faithful high priest in service to God, and*
*that he might make atonement for the sins of the people.*

HEBREWS 2:17 NIV

My daughter Amy has never liked sports. Anything that involved running and jumping, especially when other people might be watching, well, she would rather tidy her bedroom than indulge in that nonsense!

Her junior school had a Sports Day every year, and every year I took the day off work to attend. Time and again she would come in with the stragglers. I would cheer the effort, then suggest she might run faster if she wasn't carrying such a heavy scowl. I tried to assure her that it wasn't all about the winning. She should try to win, but if she didn't, she should at least try to enjoy herself.

Her fifth-grade Sports Day was held on a beautiful

sunny afternoon with many family and friends in attendance. This time, Amy managed to come in around the middle of the pack in the 100-meter race. Then, just as I was thinking about leaving, the organizer announced that there would be a dad's race to finish the day.

"Yeah. Right," I thought as I prepared to go. But Amy caught me by the arm.

"Please, Dad! Please, please, please!"

Well, I don't know many men who can resist the pleadings of their ten-year-old daughter. Groaning internally at my foolishness, I made my way to the starting line.

Now I should explain that Amy was a late baby. The gap between her and her oldest sibling is fourteen years. That's my way of saying that I was well past my prime. Some of the dads (stripped to the waist and showing every sign of taking this event very seriously) were literally half my age.

The starting gun took me by surprise. I took a few steps and stumbled. I recovered and my macho pride took over. I was determined not to look like an old man. I summoned all my resources, demanded my muscles ignore the pain, and drove forward. . .into last place!

As I stood there gasping for breath, Amy strolled past and cheerily said, "Never mind, Dad. It's not about the winning, and at least you got to enjoy yourself."

Now, I still believe you can run a better race with a smile than with a scowl, but I also know (better than before) that you shouldn't criticize someone without first walking a mile (or running 100 meters) in their footsteps!

Most of all, I now have a better appreciation of Amy's view of sports. But I had to run that race to finally understand her perspective. Jesus took part in the human race for the same kind of understanding. We might not always enjoy the journey down here on earth. But we keep on going—with a smile if we can—knowing that when He cheers us across that heavenly finishing line we will be a winner!

# If One Picture's Worth a Thousand Words. . .

GAYLE LINTZ

*Perfume and incense bring joy to the heart,*
*and the pleasantness of a friend springs*
*from their heartfelt advice.*

PROVERBS 27:9 NIV

My dad had a friend at work who was a photography hobbyist. He had worked over the years developing a good eye and some skill. He even was the photographer at my wedding.

When our first child was on the way, Ralph sat down with my dad for a serious conversation. "Dave," he said, "you've got this new baby coming. You're going to want a good camera."

Dad had always enjoyed taking pictures. My sister's and my growing-up years are well documented in photo albums. By the time we were young teens, we had cameras of our own. But Dad had never moved from "casual shutterbug" to "serious" photographer, until that fateful introduction to the world of single-lens reflex cameras and all their accessories.

Dad and Ralph went straightway to the camera store. Dad bought a camera, a flash attachment, film, and a camera bag. He went home and spent weeks learning and practicing and was completely ready by the time Kevin was born. Over the next years, with Ralph's encouragement, he bought two more high-quality cameras and a variety of lenses, tripods, and camera bags. Ralph was always ready to look at the pictures Dad took and to share advice and techniques.

Eventually, there were five grandchildren, and enough photos to wallpaper the house, inside and out. But that was just the beginning.

After Dad's retirement, he and Mom took short trips every spring, driving down back roads looking for wildflowers. They found bluebonnets and Indian paintbrush growing by barns, entwined with old rail fences, and covering acres of fields. We have pictures.

Every year, they took a big trip, like attending the LA Olympics, following the Oregon Trail, visiting Alaska. We have pictures.

Sometimes, Dad combined one of those annual trips with other interests of his, like Civil War history. Oh, do we have pictures!

One year, after one of those trips, he brought home thirty-six rolls of film, with thirty-six photos per roll. That's 1,296 pictures, and about half of them were of cannons at Revolutionary and Civil War battlegrounds. I sat with him and looked at each and every photo.

As we talked about the trip (and the cannons and the battles), he said that the most remarkable thing was the way many tourists visited the sites. "They would just drive up and park," he said. "They'd get out of their cars, walk up to the edge of the battlefield, maybe spend a few minutes at an information center. Then, they'd take a couple of pictures, and get back into their cars." He looked at his wonderful (and huge) stack of pictures. "It was something to see," he mused.

My dad wrung every bit of enjoyment out of everything he did. He learned, he studied, he planned, and he took pictures—lots of them. Often, while reliving past events by looking through his boxes and albums of photographs, he'd smile and say, "I sure am glad Ralph made me get a good camera."

# PROBLEM SOLVING
# THE MANLY WAY

P. REGINALD LEGUME

*In the spring, at the time when kings go off to war. . .*
2 SAMUEL 11:1 NIV

Our modern world. Lovely, isn't it? One minute you're on top of it. The next minute, *wham!* It's on top of you. Do you have problems? I have a few. Jesus said, " 'In this world you will have trouble,' "[1] and as you know—He was right.

As a dad, it's important to ask the right questions. The real question facing dads today is not, "Do you have problems?" but, "How do you go about solving them?" Let's analyze this conundrum carefully, rationally, and with godly wisdom.[2]

First, we'll take a quick look at how women solve problems. I won't dwell on this subject at length, because—as you and I both know so very well—women don't really have any problems!

---

1. John 16:33 NIV.
2. But not in *this* book, my friend!

However, on those rare occasions when a woman, through circumstances beyond her control, finds that she *does* have a problem—say for example, she realizes she received a lovely gift from one of her friends over a week ago and, through no fault of her own, forgot to write a thank-you note—what does she do?

Does she panic? No way! She immediately writes *two* thank-you notes, three letters of apology, purchases four lovely gifts, takes her friend out to breakfast, lunch, dinner, the movies, and, well, you get the picture. In a word, she carefully considers her problem, searches God's Word for guidance, searches *her heart* to see if anything is amiss, and then after careful thought and much prayer she does something commendable to make amends.

Way too much work.

How do *men* solve problems? Men solve problems the easy way: *by making things worse!*

Not as efficient, but definitely a lot more interesting.

Let's face it. War was invented by men. It was invented by men to solve problems quickly.

Yes, the modern man avoids the whole messy subject of searching the scriptures, thinking, praying, and considering the feelings of others by (what else?) building guns, bombs, tanks, battleships, and—when all else fails—punching as hard and as often as humanly possible.

This one simple procedure solves pretty much every problem almost immediately!

Sure, it can lead to all sorts of *other* problems. But

those new problems can always be solved by building more guns, bombs, tanks, and battleships, so no biggie.

There's just no denying it. A man's DNA is wired[3] to solve problems quickly, easily, and without thinking. Which is exactly why Jesus had to endure the most awful kind of problem solving at the hands of manly, spiritual geniuses much like myself.

Has someone or something dumped all over you? Are you locked, loaded, and ready to fire? Here's something Jesus has been trying to pound into my big numskull lately: I can't—and don't need to—fix everything. . . because He can!

> *"I have told you these things, so that in me you may*
> *have peace. In this world you will have trouble.*
> *But take heart! I have overcome the world."*
> JOHN 16:33 NIV

---

3. Replacement parts sold separately.

# TOOK AN ATTITUDE

## CONOVER SWOFFORD

*Let your conversation be gracious
and attractive so that you will have
the right response for everyone.*
COLOSSIANS 4:6 NLT

Mark was astonished when he was called by his four-year-old daughter's preschool teacher. The teacher told Mark that Brandi hit a little boy in her class. Mark couldn't believe it, because Brandi had never shown any signs of aggression. Mark picked Brandi up from school. He waited until they got home and then asked her, "Why did you hit Billy?"

Brandi put her little hands on her hips and said to her father, "Billy took an attitude with me."

"What do you mean he took an attitude?" Mark asked her.

"I told him to come play with me and he wouldn't," Brandi explained.

"You can't hit someone for not playing with you," Mark told her.

Brandi looked at him and said, "Okay. Then when *can* I hit him?"

Most of us know people who have taken an attitude with us. The question is: What attitude do we take with them? The Bible says we are to be peacemakers (Matthew 5:19). Making peace is an action. It is proactive. But how do we make peace? We make peace with our attitudes. If we have a peaceful attitude when the world around us is chaotic, people will notice. Our peaceful attitude will influence others, especially our children. When they see how we trust God to give us His peace, they will learn to trust God, too.

We make peace with our words. Proverbs 15:1 (NKJV) says, "A soft answer turns away wrath, but a harsh word stirs up anger." When someone uses words to try to provoke us, if we answer him calmly instead of angrily, our answer to him can make peace.

We make peace by pleasing the Lord. Proverbs 16:7 (NKJV) says, "When a man's ways please the LORD, He makes even his enemies to be at peace with him." When we follow God's will and plan for our lives, God Himself will make peace for us.

We grow up reading about superheroes. We admire their strength and their zeal for justice. We applaud when they outwit the villains. So, when it comes to dealing with other's attitudes, we wish we had the strength of a superhero. We want to be people who don't react poorly or say the wrong thing. Where do we get the strength to resist reacting to bad attitudes?

Jesus is our example. Jesus faced opposition, torture, and horrible attitudes. He was ridiculed and made fun of by religious leaders. Despite these difficult attitudes, Jesus responded with kindness, and with love. We are blessed that we have His example to follow. And, we are blessed to be that same example for those around us. . . for our children, our family, and our close friends.

Ask your heavenly Father to arm you with superhero strength today!

# Doin' the Dad Boogie: Celebration

*You can tell a lot about a fellow's character by his way of eating jelly beans.*
RONALD REAGAN

# GOLF

GAYLE LINTZ

*When pride comes, then comes shame;*
*but with the humble is wisdom.*
PROVERBS 11:2 NKJV

My dad played golf. He got his first golf clubs when he was in law school, early in my parents' marriage. He may not have been over-the-edge fanatic, but he did love his golf game. As far back as I can remember, he played golf every Saturday morning. Over the years, he found guys who played with similar skill and enthusiasm. He bought better clubs. His game improved. He got supplies that helped him play in a variety of situations, like long johns for cold weather, a huge golf umbrella for the wet days, and a cover-everything vinyl rainsuit for the extremely wet days. (Well, maybe he was a little bit over-the-edge.)

In Central Texas, golf is pretty much a year-round sport. But, maybe not *every* week of the year. One very cold Saturday, my dad put on his heaviest golf clothes, ate a good warm breakfast, and prepared a thermos of hot coffee to take along. He drove down the quiet early-Saturday morning streets to the course where he and his golfing buddies had planned to play. When he drove into the parking lot, he was surprised to see only one other car there, and it wasn't one of his friends. He walked into the clubhouse and greeted the astonished clerk. "I guess the rest of my group is running late," he said.

"Mr. Goodwin," said the clerk, "you can't play golf today."

"Why not?" asked Dad.

"Because the greens are frozen!"

Greatly disappointed, my dad drove back home.

While winters are mostly mild, summers can be unbearable, with afternoon temperatures over a hundred. But, to serious golfers, that doesn't mean taking time off. For Dad and his golfing pals, it meant heading off to the golf course in the dark, to be there for a 6:30 a.m. tee time.

After retiring, Dad stopped playing golf on Saturdays. That's when all the young guys played, and tee times were limited. So he and his golfing buds switched to Tuesday and Friday mornings. The local courses weren't nearly as crowded on those days.

He called once and asked me to make a document on our computer. "Ray shot his age last week," he said. "We want to present him with a certificate." I created the document, with name, date, and score, and delivered it to him. "Thanks," he said. "It's perfect. Ray'll get a big kick out of it." Then he sighed. "I might shoot my age someday. . .if I'm still playing golf when I'm ninety."

My dad never did shoot his age, but that's not why he kept on playing. He wasn't interested in showing off, being better than other players, or even having a certificate. He did work hard on his game, watching professionals, reading golf magazines, and playing often. But he really golfed for the joy of it—spending time with friends, being outdoors, and getting some exercise. What a wise example.

# FATHER'S DAY IN CHURCH (AN EXTRAVAGANT EXAGGERATION)

P. REGINALD LEGUME

*"Honor your father and your mother, so that you may live long in the land the LORD your God is giving you."*

EXODUS 20:12 NIV

Father's Day—it's almost here! That magical day in a man's life where his kids and his wife buy him a lot of expensive presents, take him out to a fancy restaurant, and then hand him the bill.

In a lot of ways, Father's Day is a lot like Mother's Day (HA!). Unless, of course, you happen to find yourself in church, which is what I would like to examine today. Let's compare the two:

## MOTHER'S DAY IN CHURCH

It's Mother's Day. . .spring is in the air! Time to pack all those screaming, rebellious little munchkins into the car and head off for a relaxing morning at church.

So what does Mom get on her special Sunday?

She gets a beautiful flower! She gets to hear a tender, encouraging, heartfelt sermon extolling the blessings of a godly mother. Everyone stands to applaud her love, grace, dedication, hard work, and beautiful, shiny hair. Then, after wiping away tears of joy, she and everyone else in her extended family are whisked away to Cracker Barrel where they have a wonderful, relaxing meal, and—as previously stated—Dad is handed a bill from the gift shop for nine thousand three hundred seventy-eight dollars.[1]

Now let's take a look at:

## FATHER'S DAY IN CHURCH

So what does Dad get on *his* special Sunday? *He gets yelled at for forty-five minutes,*[2] *of course!* Then, just as he's about ready to crawl into a Dumpster and curl up in the fetal position, Dad is handed a helpful little book (like the one you're reading right now!) filled with expert advice from godly men (like myself) who actually *know* how to raise a normal, well-adjusted, lemon-scented family (no comment). These helpful brothers in Christ remind Dad in no uncertain terms that he could *definitely* be doing a much better job, and he better get busy doing it right now or *no more Cracker Barrel for you,* you good-for-nothing, golf-club swinging, lard-covered old toot.

---

1. And sixty-two cents.
2. Or until the Pastor's head explodes, whichever comes first.

But does the fun end there? Not for good old Dad, it doesn't! After packing his precious little angels into the car and driving them safely home, dad gets to cut the grass, wash the car, walk the dog, trim the hedges, prune the trees, clean the gutters, replace the screen door, tar the driveway, paint the kitchen, fish Malibu Barbie out of the septic tank,[3] and, if he's been a *really* good boy, get stung by bees.

Now, as my wife will gladly tell you (assuming you don't actually *ask* her) I'm not one to complain. But being a dad is my favorite thing. I have a beautiful wife and two great kids who, even though they're pretty much all grown-up, still like to play with me once in a while. You can't buy *that* at Cracker Barrel or *anywhere else*.

That's the best Father's Day gift any dad could ever receive!

---

3. Again.

# I Am Soooo Tired. . .

## Paul Muckley

*The sleep of a laborer is sweet.*
Ecclesiastes 5:12 niv

True story: As a young child, I thought my parents never slept.

Somehow, they were always up and about before I rolled out of bed for the day. And they were always still going when I retired at night.

My children have no such misperceptions of me.

Like a big greasy cheeseburger or a hot fudge brownie sundae, sleep is one of the exquisite pleasures of my life. When God knit this guy together in his momma's womb, He both hardwired and programmed me to need plenty of rest.

If you're one of those type A/aggressive/purpose-driven/lion-like guys who sleeps fifteen minutes a night and always achieves each of his one-, five-, ten-, and two hundred-year goals, let me say, with all the Christian love I can muster, you make me sick.

I'd love to accomplish all you do. And I think I have

at least most of the smarts required. What's lacking, sadly, is the energy.

Given my young sons' energy, I'm convinced I could be President of the United States. Or maybe Supreme Commander of the entire Milky Way galaxy.

But no. . .God made me quieter, slower, more relaxed than a lot of other guys. And then He gave me kids.

I have a theory that active, busy children actually absorb energy from the more passive adults in their lives. The kids get wilder and crazier as the grown-ups slowly deflate like a leaking balloon. I'd test my theory scientifically, but just the thought of all that work makes me tired.

So my kids often see dear ol' Dad laid out flat. Truly, naps are beautiful things—to be enjoyed AFAP (as frequently as possible). On occasion, I might actually beat the kids to bed at night.

But there are drawbacks to sleeping when the kids are awake. Ever had an experience like this?

Six-year-old boy, excitedly: "Dad. Dad! *DAD!* Are you awake?"

Forty-something dad, groggily: "Well, son, I am now. . ."

That's kind of the way I finally learned that my own parents slept, too. I recall, at some point in childhood, padding into their room in the wee hours of the night, standing at their bedside and saying, "Mom, I think I'm gonna throw up."

And I recall Dad, bolting upright and commanding,

"Well, don't just stand there—get to the bathroom!"

Ah, memories.

Sometimes—often, really—I wish I had more energy for my kids. I'd like to wrestle more, bicycle more, hike more, swing, color, punt, pass, and kick more. And I generally experience a certain amount of guilt as I sneak in those blessed forty winks.

But, doggone it, if the Bible says a laborer's sleep is "sweet," who am I to argue? Fatherhood is undoubtedly labor, and God Himself (our "dear heavenly Father") set the precedent of resting after work.

Come to think of it, I'm just going to enjoy my sleep. And I bet I'll ultimately be a better dad for it.

# BLESSED ANNOYANCE

## PAUL MUCKLEY

*Praise the LORD. Sing to the LORD a new song,*
*his praise in the assembly of his faithful people.*
PSALM 149:1 NIV

Whether you get the joke in this title depends largely on your age and church background.

If you grew up in many Christian denominations in the 1970s or '80s, you'll probably recognize the wordplay on the Fanny Crosby hymn "Blessed Assurance." If you're of more recent vintage, and came through a church that called itself something like "The Place," a *hymn* is a praise-and-worship song from before praise-and-worship went cool.

Either way, "Blessed Annoyance" is a pretty good description of a father's offspring. Kids are undoubtedly one of the greatest blessings of life. Yet they can be as trying as a pop star mangling the tune of the national anthem before the World Series' first pitch.

Speaking of musical changeups, if the great sixteenth-century reformer Martin Luther had written a song for fathers trying to get uncooperative kids to bed, his classic hymn "A Mighty Fortress" could have been "A Nightly Torture."

Been there, done that, lost the sleep.

You might remember that the biblical King Saul—when he was tired and depressed—called on David, a young rock star (sorry, Goliath) to calm him with music. So, as a public service, we present the following Top 10 Variations on Beloved Hymns, Especially for Dads:

10) "I Need Thee Every Hour": The official fatherhood version is "I Need *Sleep* Every Hour"—and occasionally a nuclear-strength Excedrin.

9) "Blessed Be the Name": Come late January/early February, for many dads it's "Blessed Be the Game," now that the Super Bowl goes way after the kids' bedtime.

8) "This Is My Father's World": At times, we're all tempted to say "This Is *Your* Father's World"—so you kids better do what I say!

7) "O for a Thousand Tongues": Often becomes "O for a Thousand Bucks," as down payment toward a kid's braces, a family van, or a long, solitary fishing trip to northern Canada.

6) "For the Beauty of the Earth": Wouldn't it be sweet to say "For the Beauty of My Wife"? The trick is to find some quiet time away with her.

5) "Abide with Me": How about "Aside with Me"? As in, "Buddy, we need to discuss your behavior. . . ."

4) "Thou Didst Leave Thy Throne": For kids, this usually becomes "Thou Didst Leave Thy Clothes". . . scattered all over thy bedroom floor.

3) "Blest Be the Tie That Binds": I say "Blest Be the Glue That Binds." But I'm still seeking the brand that *really* fixes broken toys.

2) "Are You Washed in the Blood?": More typical question, "Are You Washed in the Tub?" And did you splash water all over the floor?

Of course, we're having some fun here, both at the kids' and the hymns' expense. But the Number One Beloved Hymn for Dads we'll play straight: "Happy the Home When God Is There." Second verse, not same as the first:

*Happy the home where Jesus' name,*
*Is sweet to every ear,*
*Where children early lisp His fame,*
*And parents hold Him dear.*

# HONOR, DEDICATION, AND PEAS

GLENN A. HASCALL

*"Honor your father and your mother,*
*so that you may live long in the land*
*the LORD your God is giving you."*

EXODUS 20:12 NIV

Every first day of the week we rose early, ate breakfast, put on our Sunday best, and went to church. As soon as Sunday school and the service were over, we piled back in the toboggan referred to as the family car and traveled sixty miles to have lunch with my mom's parents.

This was an era when Grandma would admit she'd been up since four in the morning cooking. Fast food meant the chickens out back. Green beans were snapped and canned in the fall. Fresh produce came from the garden, potatoes came from the cellar, and we always had an abundance to take home.

After lunch it was common for Dad to excuse himself from the dinner table and invite me to go for a drive. Our adventures took us to the remains of an old sod house my grandpa once lived in. We visited the family cemetery that was situated on the prairie within view of the fabled city of Nowhere. We climbed buttes, explored trails, and took a sled down a rather precarious hill. There was always something to see and someplace to go. For a young boy, these afternoons were as close to perfect as I could get.

Sometimes the trips would take us to a nursing home where my dad's dad lived. I would push myself around in his wheelchair or go to the community room to play shuffleboard by myself.

I always won.

My dad consistently honored my grandpa by the way he treated him. We visited often. Sometimes grandpa would talk or was simply content to listen. The stories I had heard about grandpa placed him right up there with legends like Wyatt Earp, Wild Bill Hickok, and Buffalo Bill Cody. As a young man, Grandpa was one of America's last stagecoach drivers.

I was immersed in this world every Sunday. Stories from Aunt Maude or Great Grandma Blanche, a trip to the chicken coop with Grandpa Wayne to look for eggs, a conversation with my Grandma Esther who insisted that if I didn't learn to eat peas, I would likely have lockjaw by the time I was thirty. Trips to see Grandpa Glenn who never really spoke about vegetable consumption much, and his jaws seemed to work just fine.

Family has always been important to my dad. His faithfulness in honoring his parents and my mom allows him to regularly visit nursing homes and share honor with those who have no one to visit.

There may not be a documentary dedicated to my dad, and he'd never sign up for a reality television show, but his life has always been a consistent example of sacrifice and honor. I suppose if I could find any fault with my dad it would be that he mixes his food before he eats it. If there had been a suggestion box dealing with new commandments, that subject would have been at the top of my list.

The tensions experienced among families should never decrease the value of honoring our parents. God calls us to honor, but ironically He said nothing about peas.

# WHEN YOU WERE
# JUST LIKE US

DAVID MCLAUGHLAN

*Who, being in very nature God, did not consider equality
with God something to be used to his own advantage;
rather, he made himself nothing by taking the very
nature of a servant, being made in human likeness.*

PHILIPPIANS 2:6–7 NIV

Get-togethers in our family are, thankfully, fun times with good food and relaxing company. But, sooner or later someone will start reminiscing about "the good old days." The same old stories will be trotted out, and there will usually be someone who hasn't heard them already.

At some point the littlest of my children will sit on my mom's lap and the bigger ones will gather around. "Tell us about when Dad was like us," one of them will ask.

With a smile, and no consideration at all for my dignity, Mom will oblige.

There's the story of how she once found me standing in a stream with my new leather school shoes on.

When she demanded to know what I was doing, I waded back to the stream's edge through knee-high water insisting that I only wanted to test the manufacturer's claim that they were waterproof.

There's the time she caught me walking off behind another family after a scolding. They had four kids, and I was sure they wouldn't notice one more. I was convinced they must surely be nicer to their kids than my mom and dad were to theirs. I wonder how tempted Mom was to let me go.

By this time my children are having a good laugh at their old dad. They love the story of my summer on the river. Along with some friends, I dumped four railroad ties into the water, made a raft and spent the summer cruising the river as a pirate. I learned to swim the following year!

With a disapproving expression (which falls just a fraction short of sincere) she tells how I used to walk up the inside of a sewage pipe, bent in half. Half a mile up the pipe passed under a telephone booth. There was a fresh air vent by the foot of the booth, and if you waited long enough you might hear someone making a call. Oh, the joy of making your own, dumb, contributions to someone else's phone call! We thought it was so funny, imagining people wondering where the voices were coming from!

At first I used to worry that retelling these stories might undermine my authority. And it usually does—for all of about twenty minutes. The children don't take me any less seriously when I need them to. They just delight in knowing that, once upon a time, I was a kid, too. Maybe it even helps my authority, because they know I know what it is like to walk in their shoes.

So, I smile (while cringing) and let them have their fun. I'm sure they'd stop if I disapproved. But that would be hypocritical. Why? Because I hope to do the same thing myself one day. In the sweet by and by I plan, if I can, to sit at the Lord's feet and say, "Father, tell me about when You were like me."

Those will be some good stories!

# Who's the Man?: Trusting God

*There is only one way to bring up
a child in the way he should go,
and that is to travel that way yourself.*
ABRAHAM LINCOLN

# MONEY, MONEY, MONEY

## PAUL MUCKLEY

*The love of money is a root of all kinds of evil.*
*Some people, eager for money, have wandered from*
*the faith and pierced themselves with many griefs.*

1 TIMOTHY 6:10 NIV

I keep finding money around the house.

A hundred dollar bill on the basement floor. . .a thousand bucks under the end table. . .even a cool ten thousand stashed in the junk drawer.

Sounds like a dream, except those bills are printed on pastel paper and come from the game of Life. If you're unfamiliar with that, it's a board game designed to show kids the effect of their educational and career decisions on how they'll ultimately live.

My kids play it pretty much the way I did years ago: They just stick the tiny plastic people in their tiny plastic cars and zoom them around the "path of life" on the board.

Sometimes I wonder: Over the decades the game has sold, how many of those pink and blue "people" have disappeared in the Bermuda Triangle of living room carpets? Probably enough to populate a large Asian nation where most plastic things are made these days.

I suppose the idea behind the game of Life is a good one: Work hard, make good choices, and you'll have a better chance at career success. But since it's a game based on random spins and card draws, there's no work at all—yet the various job choices and pay it suggests are warping the mind of my second-grade son.

"Dad! Can I really make $200,000 as a doctor?"

"Yes, I'm sure you could."

"Wow. . .I'm going to be a doctor!"

"Great, but that'll take a lot of work. Starting with feeding the dog."

Of our three kids, he's the one with dollar signs in his eyes. From about age five, whenever we'd dine out, he was the one expecting steak or shrimp. (Aren't kindergartners supposed to like hot dogs?) And there was that time some visitors came up our driveway in a gleaming new Cadillac Escalade. The reaction from the then three-year-old: "Dad, we should get one of those!"

*Uh, son, have you noticed the car I drive? It's a twelve-year-old Chevy Cavalier with 200,000 miles on it. There's a reason for that. . .called "lack of funding."*

Now the boy's fascinated with fishing, and regales me with stories of all he'd like to buy from the catalogs and magazines that never leave his hands. "Dad, this pole is only $198. . .this shark reel is only $456. . .*gasp*, look at this boat!"

*Buddy, that boat has a bedroom. . .it costs more than our entire neighborhood.*

Occasionally, I worry about that "love of money" thing in the boy's life. I'd hate to see him pierced through with many griefs. Lord knows he'll pierce himself often enough with his fishhooks.

But I'm also a little convicted. Though I don't think *I* love money, I might, sometimes, perhaps, put a little too much trust in it. And we all know that kids pick up on those things.

So I'm considering just eliminating the temptation—and giving all my money away. Would you like a pink thousand dollar bill?

# A+ FOR ABRAHAM

## JAMES LOW

*Some time later God tested Abraham. He said to him,*
*"Abraham!" "Here I am," he replied. Then God said,*
*"Take your son, your only son, whom you love—Isaac—*
*and go to the region of Moriah. Sacrifice him there as*
*a burnt offering on a mountain I will show you."*
GENESIS 22:1–2 NIV

Christians, particularly parents, struggle with this passage. How can God, who is love, ask such a thing of Abraham? Didn't God promise Isaac to Abraham, miraculously bringing about his birth? The loss of a child is devastating enough, but to call for it at Abraham's own hand? What is God thinking?

Reading the whole account, we have the luxury of knowing that God was testing Abraham and that He clearly did not desire Isaac's death. Considering Abraham's perspective, however, it must have been agonizing. We can see Abraham's trust in the Lord despite what he is called to do, but this doesn't dismiss the difficulty he faced in sacrificing his only son, Isaac, whom he loved.

I don't have a personal parallel that even comes close to Abraham's experience, but when I read this I find myself faced with a paradigm for parenthood that surely tests us today. I think this is where the difficulty for us really resides as we wrestle with this passage. We wonder, "Would God ever ask me to do such a thing?" Of course we know that God does not call any of us to literally sacrifice our kids, but we are worrisome when He calls us to unwavering loyalty to Himself, even and especially as it pertains to our role as a parent.

Herein lies the test. God tested Abraham to see if his love for his son outweighed his loyalty to God. He also tested Abraham's faith in this event. We can't forget that God promised countless descendents and blessings that would come from his seed, i.e. they would come from Isaac. Abraham had to believe that God would not only be faithful to His Word, but that He would also be able to fulfill it even if Abraham were to follow through with sacrificing Isaac. Thankfully, Abraham passed the test.

What about us? Is being a dad what defines us? Have we made our children our first love and our idols? Or, is our love for and loyalty to the Lord what defines us? Do we raise our children in sacrificial ways, symbolically surrendering them to Christ? Do we trust in God's goodness to preserve their well-being, or do we center our lives upon them and simply seek their safety and comfort?

For example, initially my dad didn't support me studying theology to become a pastor. He wanted me to study business instead, since it would provide a more financially stable future. It was hard for him, but in faith my father supported me, and now he sees the provision and fruit of the Lord's faithfulness as a result. He passed the test.

The truth is, we are tested every day that we're blessed to be called "dad." May we like Abraham, in loyal faith, pass the test.

# Bad Hair Day

## Conover Swofford

*Consider it pure joy, my brothers and sisters,*
*whenever you face trials of many kinds.*
James 1:2 NIV

Charlie was sitting on the sofa reading the newspaper when his five-year-old daughter, Liberty, entered the living room. Usually a cheerful child, Liberty stood in front of her father with a distressed look on her face.

"What's the matter, honey?" Charlie asked.

With a sigh, Liberty replied, "Daddy, I'm having a really bad hair day."

We think we'd be happy if bad hair was all that went wrong on any given day. However we need to realize that just like our troubles seem overwhelming to us, other people's troubles are overwhelming to them. There is a saying: Major surgery is what happens to me; minor surgery is what happens to you. We may think other people's troubles are minor compared to ours, but our troubles are minor compared to someone else's.

A man complained to God about the heavy burden he carried. God told the man, "Give Me your burden and then go into that room over there." The man gave his burden to God and went into the room. When he stepped inside, the man was amazed because the room was full of huge piles of burdens. "Look around," God told the man, "and pick out any burden in this room to be yours." The man looked and looked, and finally he saw a fairly small burden over against one wall. "I'll take that one over there," the man said to God. God smiled and said, "That's the burden you gave to Me."

God gives us examples in the Bible of how He helped people through their trials. Shadrach, Meshach, and Abednego were thrown into a fiery furnace. Is what we're going through worse than that? It's interesting that these three men refused to come out until Nebuchadnezzar made them. Why? Because Jesus was in the fire with them. When we're in our troubles, Jesus is in there with us.

Daniel was thrown into a lions' den. He didn't have any idea what was going to happen. All he knew was that he was in a hole filled with lions. God sent His angel to shut the lions' mouths and to protect Daniel. The next morning when the king came to see what was left of Daniel, he was amazed to see that Daniel was still alive. The king gave Daniel's God all the credit and commanded that from then on people would worship Daniel's God.

It's difficult to help others to trust God through their

troubles until we've trusted God through ours. Not only do our troubles make us better, but they also help us give others strength. God never gives us more than we can bear.

# PINE TREE OUCH FEST

GLENN A. HASCALL

*Trust in the LORD with all your heart
and lean not on your own understanding.*

PROVERBS 3:5 NIV

I heard the sounds of two boys coming in from the backyard. It was much quieter than usual, so curiosity called the dad.

"You should think about candy. That always makes me feel better," this was said by my son's friend, Nolan.

My son looked up at me and in a calm voice said, "I think I broke my arm, Dad." This entire scene was on the far side of peculiar.

I'm used to the exaggerated illness and injuries of childhood, so I looked down at his arm and told him I thought it looked fine. Perhaps this diagnosis is why I don't have an MD behind my name. As I bent down to look closer, his arm was shaped like the Eisenhower Tunnel near the wrist. I conceded my son's point and sent Nolan on his way.

Our hospital is just a few blocks from our home. I

met my wife, and she followed us to the medical facility.

Apparently my son had climbed an impressive pine tree in our backyard and slipped. It wasn't a long fall, but he landed wrong.

It would take two surgeries, some pins, and prayers to put his arm back together again, and today he has a significant centipede-shaped scar to remind him of the "Pine Tree Ouch Fest."

During the healing process, one of Ryan's proudest moments came when I took him to a monster truck rally and one of the drivers signed his cast. Ryan's friends thought a broken arm was a small price to pay for such a reward.

Am I the only dad who hates to see his children hurting? I've dealt with this internal frustration during a variety of surgeries, broken bones, and even flu shots.

While originally as obstinate as various farm animals (mostly involving those with either sharp teeth, horns, or an inability to reason) Ryan's road to recovery was filled with tedious exercises that drove him to distraction. I honestly thought he felt as if he were being punished for having an accident.

It took a long time for Ryan to be willing to climb the tree again. The tree hadn't changed. In fact, it was still accessible and as easy to climb as ever. However, Ryan had changed. He met disaster and could even pinpoint what had happened. His respect for the potential of pain caused him to be cautious about the climb. Today Ryan and the tree have settled their differences.

Trust is a tricky thing. Our children need to learn how and when to extend it to others. There are times when trusting others can result in a pain that may seem equal to falling out of a tree. Healing can take time. Help may be required.

God provides the best example of what it looks like to trust. He says we can trust Him with total abandon. As a dad, I get to model what trusting God looks like. Maybe when Ryan sees the trust I have in God, he'll consider trusting Him, too.

As to my flawed medical advice? Ryan still insists Mom provides the best first diagnosis. Who am I to argue against well-placed trust?

# Answer in the Form of a Question

## Paul Muckley

*Who has a claim against me that I must pay?*
*Everything under heaven belongs to me.*

### Job 41:11 NIV

A grown man can watch only so many kids' shows.

It's been a few years now, but I've seen my share of "children's programming"—and I'm still trying to *de*program. Unfortunately, they say that brain cells, once lost, never return.

The time was when *Bob the Builder* fascinated toddlers, but let's face it—Scoop, Muck, and Lofty never provided much intellectual challenge for adults. Though *Barney and Friends* shared some wonderful, age-appropriate life lessons for little ones, those songs quickly turned grown-up brains into quivering lumps of Jell-O. And I swear on my Stanley toolbox that I'd rather ram screwdrivers into my eyes than view another episode of *My Little Pony*.

But watching non-kid programming with kids can

be tough, too. Even sports broadcasts get tricky, what with all the jiggling cheerleaders and beer commercials to explain. Then there's the news—I mean, who wants to expose an impressionable kid to all the moral degeneration being discussed? And that's just from the congressional reporter.

No, I wanted a show I could *share* with my kids—something benign, yet educational. Something compelling, but not overly intense. Something syndicated, that typically airs between 7:30 and 8 p.m. Something hosted by Alex Trebek.

Yep, *Wheel of Fortune*.

Seriously, I know it's *Jeopardy*, because I'm kind of a trivia buff. I can tell you Willie Mays's career home run total (660), who preceded Abraham Lincoln as president (James Buchanan), and what the *Guinness Book of World Records* once identified as the earth's largest flower (the "stinking corpse lily". . .look it up).

So when announcer Johnny Gilbert opened the program by intoning, "This. . .is. . .*Jeopardy!*", I welcomed my three-year-old son to join me on the couch. He was going to be exposed to history, geography, biography, and answering in the form of a question.

If you're not familiar with *Jeopardy*, it's a trivia contest with a twist: Contestants are given the *answers*—and they have to respond with the appropriate *questions*. Like any true *Jeopardy* fan, I liked to shout out questions as contestants battled it out on screen:

"What is. . .quantum physics?"

"Where is. . .the Indian Ocean?"

"Who is. . .Fabio?" (A pretty good question, all by itself.)

Unfortunately, my son never could grasp the *Jeopardy* twist. As I threw out question after question, he'd look up and say, "I don't know. . .I don't know. . .I don't *know*. . ."

Some of life's questions have ready answers. But many of them—usually the big ones—don't. And we're left, like a three-year-old watching *Jeopardy*, to say, over and over, "I don't know."

Human nature often takes us beyond confusion to complaining—many times against God, like the Old Testament's Job did. But God answered *him* in the form of a question—several questions, actually—that proved to Job that God's knowledge and wisdom are greater than ours. In the end, we just need to trust His goodness.

What is. . .a good idea?

# My Sweet Time

P. Reginald Legume

*"Seek first his kingdom and his righteousness,
and all these things will be given to you as well."*
Matthew 6:33 NIV

If you're a person, please don't take this personally. But I—like you—am deeply flawed. Okay, I'm probably not quite as bad as you, but I *am* trying. So what does the modern dad do when he realizes his spiritual life is on the skids, and he's in need of some real help?

Does he run to the Bible for strength, comfort, and wisdom? Does he fall to his knees and seek the Lord's face?

No way!

He looks for some other poor doofus who's at least ten times worse! I mean, come on! How else are you supposed to feel better? Sharing your personal trials, tribulations, and failures with someone who is *way* worse than you are[1] is the very essence of what we dads like to refer to as "accountability."

---

1. But who is covering it up much better!

I experience times of confusion and perplexity often.[2] A couple of years ago I found myself at one of these spiritual low points. Fortunately I have a Christian friend who is always willing to listen. Why? I can't say for sure. Perhaps he's deaf. But my friend—and I'll just refer to him here as "Kim" to protect his true identity—is the real deal.

He's the kind of guy every Christian man longs to be, and I mean that sincerely. Godly. Even tempered. Deeply into the Word. A true worshipper. Great dad. Great husband. Strong. Steady. Kind. Always ready to help. A missionary at heart and a man of prayer.

I hate his stinking guts. (Okay, not really!)

But he answers his phone. So I called him up and began to spill my gooey entrails all over his beautiful Monday morning. After about ten solid minutes of whining and complaining[3] about everything under the sun, I stopped to take a quick breath, and heard him say, "My time with the Lord has been really sweet lately."

I hung up the phone.

He definitely made me think. And what did I think? You guessed it: *Well good for you and your sweet time with the Lord!*

But Kim was right. I was out of the Word. I wasn't taking time to pray. And, just like it always does when I decide I'm "too busy for that stuff," everything in my lifewas beginning to jump the tracks and roll happily down the hill and into the river.

---

2. But only while I'm awake, so no biggie.
3. Who, me?

How about you? Have you been in the Word yet today? Did you take some time to pray? Are you feeling a little mixed up, grumpy, or maybe even empty? Seek *first* His kingdom and His righteousness. He'll add every good thing when you do.

# SHORT-TERM MYSTERIES

## DAVID McLAUGHLAN

*The king said to Daniel, "Surely your God is the God of
gods and the Lord of kings and a revealer of mysteries,
for you were able to reveal this mystery."*
DANIEL 2:47 NIV

You will never meet a kid more excited about addition
and subtraction than Josh.

It was like the world of learning opened up for him.
He wanted to know more.

He would count toys, tennis balls, and place mats
and then he would take some away and re-count to
see if the resulting number matched the one he had in
his head. Learning, and trying to stump others, clearly
brought him joy.

I could tell by his expression that he thought he had a
question that might challenge the greatest philosophers—
but he was prepared to give his old dad a try.

"You can't take a bigger number away from a smaller
number." His eyes got wider with the thought. "Can you?"

Mmmmm. The easy answer was to say no, but I

knew that after a few more years at school he would learn about negative numbers. Maybe I just didn't want him to be taken by surprise. Or, more likely, I just wanted to show off!

So, I quickly outlined how you could take, say, seven away from three, by going negative. The answer would be minus four.

Having impressed my son mightily, I forgot all about it.

Parent's Night arrived, and my wife and I went to see Josh's teacher. She had good things to say about our boy, and she expected great things from him. We tried not to agree too enthusiastically.

As we stood to leave and shook her hand she dropped the bomb.

"And which of you," she asked, "do I have to thank for having to explain negative numbers to a class of first graders?"

At first I didn't get it. My loyal wife turned straight to me.

"Ahh! Well. . ."

The teacher recounted how she had explained to the children that you always took the smaller number away from the bigger number. It wouldn't work if, for instance, you took four away from three.

Josh's hand had shot up immediately. He told the whole class the answer would be minus one.

The teacher couldn't tell him he was wrong—but she couldn't tell him he right either. The rest of the class wasn't ready for that kind of math.

She and my wife slowly shook their heads in synchronized despair.

D'oh! I should have waited. It was too much information way to early in Josh's education. If I had left a little short-term mystery in his arithmetic it might have avoided a lot of confusion.

The walk of faith is full of short-term mysteries, some of which we understand with a bit more experience, or after a few years, and some of which will only be explained in the next life.

Eventually, we will understand. God has all the answers. And, unlike some earthly fathers, He prefers to share them with us at the right time.

# WHO DOES A DAD FOLLOW?: LETTING JESUS LEAD

*My father didn't tell me how to live;*
*he lived, and let me watch him do it.*
CLARENCE B. KELLAND

# DADZILLA

## P. REGINALD LEGUME

*"Can you pull in Leviathan with a fishhook*
*or tie down its tongue with a rope?"*
JOB 41:1 NIV

There's no reason to deny it. You know he's in there.
Sasquatch. The Loch Ness Monster. Donald
Trump. They all have one thing in common. They're
all legendary, larger that than life[1] figures you wouldn't
want to meet in a dark alley—or even in a well-lit but
poorly ventilated conference room, elevator, or booth
at your favorite Mexican restaurant. . . .

So why on earth would I bring up such a troubling
subject in a lighthearted, humor-infested book such as
this? *How should I know?*

As a young child I became frightened very easily. And
in those impressionable, formative years where my future
psyche teetered on the verge of wrack and ruin, one of
the most terrifying movies my parents ever forced me to

---

1. Or at least their hair is.

watch over and over and over again was—you guessed it—*Rudolph the Red-Nosed Reindeer.*

I doubt there were many manly, young men who had to hide behind their dad's La-Z-Boy during Rudolph. But—and I kid you not—I was definitely one of them. What unearthly, uninvited, unexpected, *ungodly* creature could possibly be so terrifying that it filled my tiny, impressionable heart with such unreasonable terror, dread, and woe?

Just think about it for a second. The wild, stringy white hair. The unearthly, pale blue lips. The bulging, twirly crossed eyes. *The claws! The fangs!* The great, big, hairy, white back! I'm talking about:

*THE BUMBLE!*

Ooooooooh. Tell me when it's over!

Yes, I was terrified of The Bumble. But I've gotten over it. Now that I'm older, that's pretty much exactly how I look when I roll out of bed in the morning. But while it's one thing to *look* like a monster, it's another thing *entirely* to realize you're beginning to act like one. As you know, even we well-meaning Christian dads who have (hopefully) put all this scary business behind us once and for all, can now and again unintentionally regurgitate the wild-eyed, partially digested remains of our pre-Christian selves all over our unsuspecting friends and family.

You know what I'm talking about. . .

He's big. He's ugly. He smells like bad cheese. He's. . . *Dadzilla!*

You try to keep him buried, but he keeps popping out of the ocean[2] to stomp all over your best efforts to become the kind of dad you know you long to be.

So tell me, have you been flaming everyone with that big, green, monster mouth of yours lately?

I still do it every now and then.

Does it do anyone any good? I don't know. It sure doesn't feel like it—at least not to me. I *am* sure of this though: The blood of Jesus bound my Dadzilla up and locked him away for good. But it's up to me to keep my hands off the dungeon door when he wakes up and decides he wants to come out and play.

---

2. Can anyone say, "family vacation"?

# MY (SON'S) HERO

PAUL MUCKLEY

*He has shown you, O mortal, what is good.*
*And what does the LORD require of you?*
*To act justly and to love mercy and*
*to walk humbly with your God.*

MICAH 6:8 NIV

L.L.Bean, how dare you?

Come to think of it, if I'm going to tackle a large, powerful American retailer, perhaps I should be more circumspect. Let's say, hypothetically, we're discussing a well-known "outfitter" in the "northeast United States" that we'll call "L.L.Spleen."

That should satisfy the legal department as I return to my rant.

Actually, I *like* L.L.Bea—oops, "Spleen." I've purchased lots of outdoor stuff from them—hiking shoes, biking pants, Viking helmets.

But this large, powerful, well-known outfitter crossed a line when it sent me a thick catalog about fishing. I'm no animal rights fanatic—I love the bumper sticker that says PETA: People Eating Tasty Animals—I just don't care to fish. My eight-year-old son, unfortunately, does—and devoured that catalog, driving me half crazy with questions about rods, reels, lures, and lines. Of course, I didn't have a clue how to answer.

One time (actually, many, *many* times), my son asked me to decipher the following gobbledygook from the L.L.Spleen catalog. As the powerful, well-known American humorist Dave Barry (or rather, "Dave Splarry") says, "I am not making this up":

WF-F 3-7 Chartreuse 90'

Huh?

*Son, I wish you were half as intrigued by your schoolwork.*

What I really wish is that I could share his enthusiasm. But fishing just isn't my thing. . .and hunting? Don't get me started on Cabelas. Sorry, "Splabelas."

Though I love the outdoors, I don't feel a need to yank fish out of their habitat or drop large animals with a shoulder-mounted howitzer. Nothing against the guys who do. But if I want meat, I'll get it the way God intended—wrapped in plastic at the local supermarket.

For heaven's sake, I work as an editor. The struggle this somewhat bookish dad faces is how best to serve a red-blooded American boy whose interests often diverge—wildly—from my own.

"Hey, son. . .let me show you how to edit a manuscript."

"Gee, Dad. . .can't we just rent a boat and go ocean fishing?"

"Um, buddy, we live in Ohio. Here, can I show you how I outline a book?"

"Could we go to Africa to hunt elephants?"

Boys want heroes and dads want to *be* heroes. Early in life, we're heroic just by being there. But as time goes on, personal interests and style often create a divide—maybe a crack in the pavement, maybe the Pacific Ocean—between us dads and the boys we love.

So what's a guy to do when he's a jock and his kid's a computer geek? Or when dad's a hard-nosed businessman and his kid's a cream puff? Or, in the widest chasm of all, what if dad's kid is a *girl*?

Thankfully, we don't always have to "get" our kids to be good fathers. We just need to set a consistent example of fairness, mercy, and love for God.

That's better than fishing any day.

# Prejudiced

## Conover Swofford

*Do not hold the faith of our Lord Jesus Christ,
the Lord of glory, with partiality.*
JAMES 2:1 NKJV

On their way to church one Sunday morning, ten-year-old Jason asked his father, "Daddy, are we prejudiced?"

Startled, his father said, "Son, why would you ask me that?"

"Well," said Jason, "I just wanted to know if we are prejudiced or Methodist or what religion we are."

Unfortunately there is prejudice in this world. If we show prejudice, our children will show prejudice. Prejudice is an insidious evil. It sneaks into our lives in all sorts of ways, and we have to be careful to guard against it. Prejudice isn't just about race, religion, or gender; it can show itself in our disdain for a homeless person or in our fear when a stranger walks toward us. In response to this, the author of Hebrews encourages believers to "Do not neglect to show hospitality to strangers, for by this some have entertained angels without knowing it" (Hebrews 13:2 NASB).

It's uncanny (and a little scary) how much our children imitate us. Everything we do influences our children, and the "do as I say and not as I do" philosophy has little effect on them. They watch what we do and how we behave much more than they ever listen to what we say. So, when they see us loving our neighbors, they'll know that they should love their neighbors. When they see us sharing the gospel, they'll want to share the gospel, too.

God extends His grace to all, and we can do no less. In fact, we have no right to withhold His grace from anyone. As we pass through this world, we must spread the message of the love and grace of God. James makes it crystal clear in the verse above, we are to do with without partiality. We don't get to pick and choose who we share God's message with. Jesus died for all. That's everyone!

Any person we meet is sent to us by God. There are no chance encounters in God's world. God put us here to be examples for others, to be good teachers and good parents. If we want our children to be strong believers, we must demonstrate that for them. How should we raise them? Proverbs reminds us to "Start children off on the way they should go, and even when they are old they will not turn from it" (Proverbs 22:6 NIV). That training starts with us as we follow the Lord and set an example for our children.

# DADS OF DEUTERONOMY

## JAMES LOW

*These commandments that I give you today are
to be on your hearts. Impress them on your children.
Talk about them when you sit at home and when you walk
along the road, when you lie down and when you get up.*

DEUTERONOMY 6:6–7 NIV

Every so often I catch myself reminiscing about "the good ole days." You know, the carefree days of our younger years when the responsibilities of life seem to be a distant "blip" on the radar. My best friend Tommy and I often spent these days creating various projects to occupy our time.

We spent countless hours restoring his parents' old MGB with dreams of racing it around town. We spent weeks trying to catch the world's biggest fish at the local fishing hole. In fact, it seems the only breaks we took from fixing up the old car and fishing was to work on a kayak that Tommy and his dad started making from scratch. To be honest, Tommy did most of the work and I often just watched, wondering if it would float.

Regardless of what we were working on, Tommy's dad was always there to help out and give us advice. What I didn't realize at the time was that Tommy's dad would also somehow steer our conversations toward "God." During dinner, sitting around a campfire, in the car on a road trip, or often over his famous chocolate chip pancakes, Tommy's dad would read the Bible or recite a passage that was on his heart following it up with something like, "What do you think?"

Thinking back, I see how these conversations impacted Tommy and me. Tommy's dad had a strong relationship with the Lord, and he spoke about that relationship with us often. Those conversations shaped our own relationships with the Lord as we learned that the Lord's love and work were not far removed from the everyday aspects of life. In fact, it was these conversations that helped transform a "father's faith" into our own.

The words of Deuteronomy above are important. Moses is speaking to the Israelites, calling them to faithfulness to God's law, and to share it with their children as they live their lives together. We need to remember that the backdrop for the giving of God's law is His rescue of the Israelites from slavery in Egypt. Only after this does God instruct His people about how they should live. Moses, knowing that obedience to the law is the only right response to God's redeeming love, is calling parents to recognize this and to teach their children God's law in light of the reality of God's sovereignty and grace. In doing so, they and their children can look forward to the consummation of God's promised covenant blessings.

Following Moses' instruction, Tommy's dad, himself having been delivered by God's grace, sought to live his life according to God's will, teaching us along the way why following God was important. Surely this is the will of God for those of us blessed to be called "dad."

# Follow the Leader

## Conover Swofford

*Follow my example, just as I follow the example of Christ.*

1 Corinthians 11:1 niv

Amos asked his four-year-old son, Christian, "Why do you always have to be the leader when we play Follow the Leader?"

Christian replied, "When I was born, they told me I was the leader, and all the other children would follow me."

"Is that so?" Amos asked with a smile.

"Yep," Christian replied with confidence.

Christian wasn't wrong. Leadership is one of the gifts God gives to certain people. It is an awesome responsibility, and God expects us to use it wisely. In order to be good leaders, we must be sure we are leading our followers in the right direction—and that means leading them to the Lord. We do this is by learning to know God personally, learning to understand His activity in our lives and expressing His love to others. God says that if we trust Him, He will direct our paths

(Proverbs 3:6). In order to lead, we have to follow. We follow where God leads us, and as we do, the ones following us go in the same direction. Even if we're not the designated leader, other people watch us. As Christians we are under constant scrutiny by the world. We need to make sure that what they see in us points them to God.

God expects fathers to be leaders in their homes. The list of qualifications for leaders given in 1 Timothy includes "He must manage his own family well and see that his children obey him, and he must do so in a manner worthy of full respect" (1 Timothy 3:4 NIV). Samuel was a mighty man of God, but his sons ran amok. Aaron was God's high priest, and two of his sons were killed for offering strange fire in the tabernacle. Leaders must be careful that they are not so focused on their ministries that they neglect their children.

Our children mimic our behavior, and sometimes repeat things we have said that we might not want to hear repeated. A father was taking his three-year-old son trick or treating. He was trying to get his son to say, "Thank you," whenever he received candy from someone. At one house, after the son had received candy, the father said, "What do you say?" The son looked at the woman who was their neighbor and said, "Daddy says your dog is ugly." The embarrassed father mumbled an apology and took his son away.

In Ephesians 6:4 fathers are specifically admonished against provoking their children to wrath. It is easier to say, "Because I said so," than it is to take time to explain or reason with our children. God has given them inquiring minds, and we are to teach them the ways of the Lord. We are to teach them by example, not just with words. As important as it is to memorize scripture, it is equally important to apply those scriptural principles to our lives.

# THE NEXT GENERATION

JAMES LOW

> *"I, the LORD your God, am a jealous God,*
> *punishing the children for the sin of the parents*
> *to the third and fourth generation of those who hate me,*
> *but showing love to a thousand generations of those*
> *who love me and keep my commandments."*
>
> EXODUS 20:5–6 NIV

Some read this verse thinking, "How unfair. How can God punish children for their parents' sin?" Others wonder what it means for God to be jealous, but only get far enough to conclude that one generation's sin definitely doesn't justify the punishment of subsequent generations. Looking at the verse from this perspective, however, some important things are easily overlooked. Reading more carefully we see that God punishes the children to the third and fourth generation, for the sin of the parents who are identified as those who hate God. We also see God showing love not just to the third and fourth generations, but to a thousand generations.

Something needs to be said in regards to this "love

and hate" language. Both have their home in the realm of relationship, but they don't limit themselves to the emotive understanding that the modern reader associates them with. From a biblical perspective, "love and hate" have more to do with loyalty than with emotion. Hate describes disloyalty expressed by disobedience. Love is likened with loyalty and is expressed by obedience. This is evidenced in our passage. Sin and hate, being paired together, are contrasted with the pairing of love and keeping commandments.

The question, "How can God punish the children and subsequent generations for the disobedience of their 'hateful' parents?" remains. A lesson from Christian counseling helps us discover an answer. Research and practice has long testified to the immense impact that parents and families have in the formation of their children. It is now considered common knowledge that subsequent generations typically follow the patterns of their parents.

Though it has taken us considerable time to find this out, God has always known it, and He pleads with us as parents to recognize it. Though it isn't always the case that parents who love God and loyally obey Him will have children who love and are loyal to God, we would be foolish not to regard the parental patterns that shape the future of our families. God in His wisdom graciously reveals to us the important role that we have as parents.

The questions this passage produces aren't put to God, but to us as parents, particularly dads. As the heads of our households, do we live lives where our love for God is expressed in obedience to Him, or are we living in sinful disobedience as if we hate Him? Do we educate our children about living a right relationship with God, seeking to know and obey His will as a response to having received His grace and forgiveness through Jesus Christ? The weight of such questions is felt when we consider that our answers impact not only our children, but also our children's children, and on to the next several generations.

# Hardheaded

## Paul Muckley

*Consider it pure joy, my brothers and sisters,*
*whenever you face trials of many kinds.*
JAMES 1:2 NIV

My kid is really hardheaded. Literally speaking.

Oh, he shows some hardheadedness in the figurative sense, too—but I'm thinking of that big, solid wrecking ball on the north end of his neck. Yeah, it's that kind of a head.

Even as an infant, while taking milk from a bottle, he'd whip that heavy thing around and conk my wife or me on the nose, the chin, or the cheekbone. In toddlerhood, the head sought out our shins, knees, and thighs like some sort of heat-seeking missile. It was a kind of self-propelled sledgehammer, wreaking havoc on any unsuspecting soft tissue in its path.

So one day, when the three-year-old head tumbled down our basement stairs, we were amazed that it didn't crack the floor. Actually, the scoreboard read CONCRETE 1, HEAD 0 as Mr. Wrecking Ball became Mr. Retching

Barf, a classic sign of concussion.

And not *only* a concussion—our first parental ER trip came with a diagnosis of skull fracture, followed by a fun (and pricey) ambulance ride to the children's hospital thirty miles north.

As parents go, we're pretty laid back. Somehow, we had always *known* we'd end up in the hospital with this kid, so we weren't overly stressed. But then the inquisition began.

If you ever take a young head injury case to the hospital, be prepared: Everyone you meet—the doctors, the nurses, the receptionists, the janitor carrying a plunger—will grill you as to what exactly happened. And just as you never say "bomb" in an airport, this is probably not a time to joke about whapping anyone "upside the head."

Of course, they're trying to make sure your story checks out. Apparently ours did—because the hospital folks' demeanor soon changed. They became very friendly. And they began sharing stories of traumatic injuries to their *own* kids:

"My daughter tried to ride the dog and fell and broke her arm."

"My son thought he was Superman and broke his ankle jumping off the roof."

"There was that time my kid shot himself out of a homemade cannon. . ."

Ultimately, the hospital kept our son for a couple of days—and he loved it. Why not? He had his own room with bright, fun decorations. . .way more channels on the TV than we had at home. . .and every couple of hours, a chance to choose stuffed animals, blankets, books—you name it—from a pleasant lady's "gift cart." The one thing she didn't carry was football helmets, but I guess you can't have everything.

Honest to goodness, at one point the boy looked at me and asked, "Dad, are we on vacation?"

*Maybe for you, son. . .*

Really, I'd like to have more of that perspective—to see the positives over the negatives of life. When troubles come (and they do), James says we can (and should) consider them "pure joy."

But that takes a conscious choice and regular practice, a soft heart over a hard head.

# Job's Job

JAMES LOW

*Job would make arrangements for them to be purified.*
*Early in the morning he would sacrifice*
*a burnt offering for each of them, thinking,*
*"Perhaps my children have sinned and cursed*
*God in their hearts." This was Job's regular custom.*

JOB 1:5 NIV

My dad's early morning custom ran like clockwork. In fact, it started with him switching off his alarm clock at 5:35 a.m., which I could hear through my bedroom wall just adjacent to my parents' bedroom. He spent no more than five minutes in the shower, about the same shaving, and then quickly donned a dry-cleaned suit before heading down the short hall to my and my brother's bedroom doors.

At about five till six he would knock as he stuck his head in and said, "Time to get up, let's go." He would continue until he saw our feet on the floor and then, and only then, would he head downstairs for a quick cup of coffee. My brother and I would use this window of opportunity to crawl back into bed for another ten to fifteen minutes, but as soon as we heard his hard-soled dress shoes walking about the kitchen and heading back to the stairs, we would spring into action before he came to say his good-byes and make sure we wouldn't miss the bus. At about six-fifteen or so he could be heard getting into his car and pulling out of the garage as he headed to work and another day on the job.

There is a lot to be said for regular routines. I've come to respect how disciplined my dad was, and I really appreciate how, day in and day out he stuck to it, helping us start our days and providing for our household. The reason I share my dad's old routine is that it makes sense. Waking up, getting ready for our day, getting the kids ready for theirs, and then heading off to work and enjoying our job just *feels* right. While such routines are good and necessary, deep down we know that the job of a dad doesn't stop here. The question, however, is not "Where does the dad's job stop?" but "Where does it start?"

Job's account helps answer this question. While we no longer need purifying sacrifices in order to live in a right relationship with God our Father, we still ought to see Job's attitude and actions here as exemplary. Job rose early in the morning, not to grab a cup of coffee before heading to work, but rather saw his "job" as focusing on his children's relationship with God and what he could do to ensure that this, above all else, was intact. This was his regular routine.

It ought to be our regular routine as well. Like Job, our job is to be disciplined in helping our children focus on their relationship with the Lord. Instead of the old practice of purifying sacrifices, we should submit ourselves to prayer for, on behalf of, and with our children. Of course our job as "dad" doesn't stop here, but that's where it should start.

# FINDING JOY
# UNDER THE SUN

GAYLE LINTZ

*So I commend the enjoyment of life,*
*because there is nothing better for a person under*
*the sun than to eat and drink and be glad.*
*Then joy will accompany them in their*
*toil all the days of the life God*
*has given them under the sun.*
ECCLESIASTES 8:15 NIV

My dad learned to play golf when he was in Baylor Law School. Someone gave him a set of clubs, and he set to work learning how to use them. He played every now and then and developed a sincere, long-lasting love for the game. When he finished law school, I know my grandmother hoped he would return to his northern Ohio home with his new wife, and settle there permanently. But my mother was loathe to leave her parents and sisters, who all lived within a hundred miles. I know there were many considerations, but I think the tipping point may have been golf. In northern Ohio, there is snow on the ground for six or seven months of the year. Golfers in Central Texas can enjoy the sport almost year-round. Whatever the reason, my mom and dad stayed in Texas. Eventually, there was enough money and time for him to play golf almost every Saturday morning.

It's great to have a golfer in the house at gift-giving time. Over the years, he got golf club head covers, golf towels, golf gloves, golf socks, golf shoe cleat cleaners, golfing magazine subscriptions, gift certificates to local golf courses, and package after package after package of golf balls and golf tees.

Every time we took a trip, the first item in the car trunk was the golf bag, filled with freshly cleaned golf clubs and shiny new golf balls (that he had recently received for Father's Day or his birthday). If there was a course anywhere near wherever we were headed, he wanted to be able to play it.

After Dad's retirement, my parents travelled quite a bit. Without me and my sister along, there was plenty of room in the backseat of the car for any bulky souvenirs they might want to purchase. There certainly wasn't an excess of space in the car's trunk. The golf supplies were there!

One summer, when they had travelled to Ohio to visit Dad's family, an uncle was wondering about Dad's plans while they were there. (You may not be able to play golf there in January, but you certainly can in July!) "Dave," he asked my dad. "Did you bring your golf clubs?" My mother looked up at my uncle, narrowing her eyes. "Did he bring me?" she shot back. A valid question.

If my dad were rewriting Ecclesiastes 8:15, he would say, "there is nothing better for a person under the sun than to spend a morning on the golf course." People should seek to find satisfaction in their work or "toil" in life. But they should surely have activities that give them joy, all the days of the life God has given them.

# LEANING ON ABBA'S ARMS: GOD'S PROTECTION

*Pray as though everything depended on God.*
*Work as though everything depended on you.*
ST. AUGUSTINE

# A Lesson in
# Laying Carpet

## Paul M. Miller

*This is your lot in life and in your toilsome labor
under the sun. Whatever your hand finds
to do, do it with all your might.*
Ecclesiastes 9:9–10 niv

Visiting one's adult children is always an eye-opener. For some reason, even though the dates on their birth certificates deny it, they are still your little kids. As I write these words, son Tim is fifty yards away laying a backyard watering system with help from his brother-in-law, daughter Lisa's husband, Ben.

Sentimentalist that I am, my mind travels back to labor-intensive projects that involved the kids in earlier days. Tim was always a driven get-it-done kind of guy. His teachers would report that he consistently threw himself into every project, whether good or not so good.

It's been a family joke that ol' Dad was much too right-brained to complete any job that involved logic or tools. Of course, he who laughs loudest will surely have his day of reckoning.

Tim's came one afternoon at a formal church wedding, for which he and another pre-teen boy were deputized to serve as carpet unrollers—a ceremony that provided a pristine aisle-covering for the bride's feet.

On cue, Tim and his cohort unrolled the whole canvas down the long aisle to the altar, then sat on the front row to watch the nuptial proceedings.

As the ceremony came to an end, I could tell Tim was wondering "Now what?" In a flash, he whispered something to his partner. Then, before the minister could begin his closing remarks, the two boys were on their knees re-rolling the white carpet back up the aisle. The sight was startling: two fellows in black tuxes on their knees, with bottoms up, attempting the near impossible—re-spooling the canvas carpet.

A shocked hush spread across the sanctuary. Tim's mother mumbled to me, "What in the world. . ."

A woman in front of us turned to her husband and declared, "Well, I never. . ."

As the boys humped up the center aisle, Pastor Wetmore watched the proceedings, then spoke in his best pulpit voice, "As the writer of Ecclesiastes wrote, 'Whatever your hand finds to do, do it with all your might.' That goes for your knees, too."

At the reception, Tim looked quite pleased with himself. "Well, we got it done," he announced to me, sipping a cup of Hawaiian Punch. "People sure thought we did a great job."

"Oh really?" I asked. "What gives you that idea?"

"Lots of people told me that we were about the *funnest* thing at the wedding."

"*Funniest*," I corrected.

"Yeah, that's what they said."

When we got home, and Tim was in normal duds, his mother asked, "What made you roll the carpet back up the aisle at the end?"

Tim's answer was quite logical, "Well, we couldn't leave it, could we? We put it down there in the first place, so it was our job to roll it back up."

Pastor Wetmore and the person who penned Ecclesiastes had it right—whatever our toilsome lot in life, for goodness' sake, we've got to do it with all our might. That was a lesson for not only Tim, but for me, too.

# JELLY BELLY BABY

*"Which of you, if your son asks for bread,*
*will give him a stone? Or if he asks for a fish,*
*will give him a snake? If you, then, though you are evil,*
*know how to give good gifts to your children,*
*how much more will your Father in heaven*
*give good gifts to those who ask him!"*

MATTHEW 7:9–11 NIV

A little over a year and a half ago our family celebrated the birth of baby Dylan. Having been blessed with daughters, Dylan's arrival was greatly anticipated by the family. You see, not only is Dylan my brother and his wife's first baby, he is also the first boy born to the family. Though the entire family is overjoyed by God's gift of Dylan, none compares to the joy of his parents.

You can see this joy exuding from my brother's face as he dotes on his now one-and-a-half-year-old son. What is most telling is the elation on Dylan's face whenever "daddy" is near. The family gets a kick out of watching them together, seeing all the smiles, hearing all

179

the laughs, and looking at all the funny faces exchanged between the two of them.

Many hours have been spent trying to figure out how to make Dylan laugh or smile. While he enjoys watching us dance, get hit in the head, or roll around like monkeys, we've discovered that the surefire way to a wide-eyed cheek-to-cheek smiley face is the presence of his favorite sweet treat, jelly beans.

Perhaps the funniest face I've ever seen Dylan make came during an instant of perplexing disappointment. As my brother and I played "blocks" with Dylan, something on top of the nearby table caught his eye. Dylan spied a bag of jelly beans, and that was all she wrote. Eyes wide open and arms outstretched, Dylan would not be distracted. He wanted a jelly bean. We pointed to everything but the jelly beans asking, "Do you want this?" To which he would respond with a groan as he reached toward the bag. After a short while, my brother consented, reached into the bag, and pulled out a bean.

Dylan could hardly contain himself and began sounding his excitement as his hand reached for his dad's. My brother, ever the jokester, held out his hand and said, "Here you go" placing one of Dylan's tiny toys into his hand. Dylan's face devolved from uncontainable happiness to devastating disappointment. He crumpled his lips and scrunched his eyebrows. Then ever so slowly, as he turned his gaze from the toy in his hand to his dad, he raised an eyebrow as if to say, "What's this?" Of course it was only a moment before my brother produced the coveted jelly bean, giving it to Dylan who devoured it with jubilant laughter.

The parallel to the passage above can't be missed. Playing on a father's provision for his son, its asks a rhetorical question to which the obvious answer leads one to see their relationship with our heavenly Father in a whole new light. We are grounded in His protection and provision. It is by His paternal love that we live. Not only do we seek to exemplify this paternal love to our children, but it is by it that we find the strength and security to be the fathers we're called to be.

# Re: Tim's Brief Career as a Pianist

## Paul M. Miller

*Patient endurance is what you need now,*
*so that you will continue to do God's will.*
*Then you will receive all that he has promised.*
**Hebrews 10:36 NLT**

For a while our son Tim did pretty well with piano lessons, especially a number from *Thompson Book One*. If you've had lessons, and are familiar with the Thompson piano method, you'll remember that's the red book.

Tim's first recital piece was out of Thompson; it was called "By a Wigwam." If I remember correctly, his teacher had penciled on the page, "Right hand mysterious, like an Indian brave tracking a deer; left hand like drumbeats."

Goodness knows how many weeks his sister and parents had to endure that left hand thumping, or the single notes of the right hand trying to sound mysterious, but never at the same time.

"Dad, I just can't make the drumbeats and the sneaking Indian brave go together."

"We've noticed."

"What would happen if at that dumb recital I'd play my left hand first, and then played my right hand?"

"It would make the piece twice as long, son."

"Yeah, and Mrs. Morsch would yell at me."

A week or two before the dreaded recital, I was having my quiet time in Hebrews, and I ran across a verse about patience and endurance. It seemed a likely scriptural boost to lay on Tim. It was also very good for the rest of us, who were enduring Tim's almost daily twenty-minute practice sessions.

"Son, let me read you something out of the Bible: 'Patient endurance is what you need now.' What do you think?"

"Patience for me. . .or for you guys?"

"Maybe both."

"We really need to let God know that you need His help."

The afternoon of the recital was bright and summery for spring. Instead of walking to Mrs. Morsch's house where the recital was held, Tim drove over with his family.

"Got your music?" his sister reminded with a nudge.

"Of course."

"You never told us what you had Mrs. Morsch write in the program about you and your piece," Tim's mom remarked.

"You'll see."

When we got to the Morsch home, there were cars in

the driveway and at the curb. I could tell the sight made Tim nervous. Walking up the front steps, he took a fast glance in the red music book and sighed.

A smiling Mrs. Morsch showed us to our chairs in the dining room. "I'm so proud of Tim," she encouraged. "You will be, too, I'm sure." Then she handed us a program.

"Don't read it now, please," Tim pleaded. "Wait'll I'm up there."

Tim was the second *Book One* pianist to perform. He followed a girl who got lost in her performance and started again. I looked over at my son. He gave me the "OK" sign with his fingers. Then it was his turn.

"I am playing 'By a Wigwam.' It is the story of an Indian boy out hunting."

As he placed his right and left hands on the keys, I opened the mimeographed program. By his name and the title of his piece, Tim had Mrs. Morsch write, "Hope everyone has patience and endures."

# How Do You Measure Success?

Paul Muckley

*"Watch out! Be on your guard against all kinds of greed; life does not consist in an abundance of possessions."*

Luke 12:15 NIV

Some guys measure success by the number of zeroes in their bank accounts. I'm just happy if my bank balance is greater than zero.

Some guys measure success by the higher horsepower of their cars. I'm really pleased by a lower horse*play* in my car.

Some guys measure success by the square footage of their homes. I don't know much about square feet—I just hope the feet in my house aren't muddy.

You might notice a theme developing here.

Some guys build thriving businesses. I build dollhouses and Lego castles.

Some guys hunt big game. I hunt for the pieces to board games.

Some guys watch the stock market. I watch a lot of animated movies.

Have you guessed I'm the father of young kids?

Some guys host Very Important People at fancy restaurants. I share hash browns and Cinnamelts at McDonalds.

Some guys have season tickets for the National Football League. I've got a lifetime pass to the National Fatherhood League.

Some guys are driven around in limousines. Many days, I'm just driven crazy.

If any of this sounds familiar, you must have some daddy-ing experience yourself.

Fatherhood is truly a mixed bag of fun and frustration, noise and joys, soaring pride and pull-out-what's-left-of-your-hair befuddlement. It's a maddening pleasure, an invigorating exhaustion, an immensely wealthy poverty in all of its oxymoronic glory.

But how do you measure success in life? How do you compare yourself to all the other men in the world?

Some guys find cures for horrible diseases. I get to clean up any barf in the house. (My wife sneaked that into our wedding vows.)

Some guys write Pulitzer prize-winning novels. I write a whole lot of checks—to the doctor, the dentist, the Cub Scouts, the softball league, the church camp, seemingly anyone who's ever had even the briefest interaction with my kids.

Some guys get elected grand poobah of their clubs,

professional associations, cities, states, and nations. I've been elected dogcatcher (and feeder, trainer, and poop scooper) of our little acre of the world, population five: me, mom, daughter, son, other son. Hey, somebody's gotta do it.

Am I a success? Not by Donald Trump's standard. Probably not even by Donald Duck's. Certainly not by Scrooge McDuck's. But I'm not sure those are the real yardsticks to measure against.

Some guys have earned all the fame and fortune this world can offer. I've earned the affection of my three young kids.

Some guys accumulate Frequent Flier Miles. I collect Frequent Child Smiles.

Some guys are so busy with work and hobbies they hardly ever see their kids. I get school lunch dates, personalized drawings, bedtime-stretching story requests, heart-melting hugs and kisses, and "I LOVE YOU, DADDY" notes sent to my phone, tucked into the pages of my Bible, and hidden around my desk.

Just how does a guy measure success? I think I've determined my standard.

What is yours?

# WHERE DO I BEGIN?

DAVID MCLAUGHLAN

*Every good and perfect gift is from above,*
*coming down from the Father of the heavenly lights,*
*who does not change like shifting shadows.*

JAMES 1:17 NIV

On our first Christmas together, it didn't matter that we didn't have much money for presents. Mandy was just a baby, and it was just another day for her.

The next year our finances weren't any better. The contract I had been working on had come to an end, and jobs were scarce. Mandy's presents that year came mostly from her grandparents, aunts, and uncles. Oh, and there was a doll's house I made from discarded wood. I painted it a rainbow of colors from old paints I found.

The following Christmas we were in better shape. When Mandy went to bed on Christmas Eve, my wife and I wrapped her presents together and piled them up on an armchair. That pile was so high you could not see the back of the chair. We decorated the whole thing with ribbons and glitter. Maybe we were going over the top, but we had some gift-famine years to make up for!

The next morning came, and I could tell by the quality of the light that it had snowed overnight. My wife and I slipped downstairs so we would be well positioned to enjoy Mandy's expression when she saw her presents.

A little while later a bleary-eyed two-and-a-half-year-old shuffled into the living room in her slippers and nightgown. An aura of cozy sleep was still wrapped around her. She rubbed an eye with the back of one hand and muttered a sleepy "Goo monnin."

She stopped in front of the armchair (we had positioned it so it would be the first thing she would see). It took a couple of seconds for the image to sink in, but as it did her arms fell down to her sides, her eyes grew wider, and she sucked in a gasp of air. She let it all out in one big, "Wowwwwww!"

And then she just stood there.

My wife and I looked at each other. Mandy stood transfixed.

"Aren't you going to open your presents, sweetheart?" I asked.

She pulled her gaze away from the glittering pile of gifts and stared at me in awestruck confusion.

"But Dad. . . ," she gasped. "Which one's mine?"

My little sweetheart had never felt shortchanged by not having many presents. She knew she was loved, and that was enough. But when a little of that love was expressed in a chair full of presents she was amazed. Delighted—but amazed!

Being a little less innocent, I occasionally do feel shortchanged. But I shouldn't. I am loved, even when I feel I'm not getting what I want. And if God was actually to wrap up and glitter all the gifts He had waiting for me, it would take more than an armchair to hold them. It would take the world! And I'd probably be speechless, too.

# THE CAKE AUCTION

CONOVER SWOFFORD

*"If you then, being evil, know how to give good gifts to your children, how much more will your Father who is in heaven give good things to those who ask Him!"*
MATTHEW 7:11 NKJV

The annual Cake Auction held at the church was one of the most eagerly anticipated events of the year. The auctioneer, Randy, came from a large family of bakers, and his mother, Jean, made the best-selling cakes.

Before the auction started, Chris, a small two-year-old boy, wandered among the tables trying to see the cakes. His head barely came to the top edge of the tables. Randy picked Chris up so that he could see better. As Randy stood holding Chris, Jean said, "I bid $200 for the boy."

"Sold!" said Chris's father. "Now what do you bid for his diaper bag?"

Everyone laughed. Randy handed Chris to Jean, and the auction began. Randy immediately made it clear that when his mother's sour cream lemon pound cake came up for auction, he would be bidding against all comers. The auction proceeded smoothly and then came Jean's pound cake. Randy immediately bid $25. Another bidder quickly bid $50. To Randy's surprise, it was his daughter, Elizabeth, bidding against him.

"Sweetheart," Randy said. "Why are you bidding against me?"

"Because if you win the cake, we won't get any of it," Elizabeth replied, grinning.

Randy looked at his daughter and said, "$75."

"$100," came his daughter's response.

"$125," Randy said.

"$150," Elizabeth topped him.

"$200," said Randy, hoping to stop Elizabeth by jumping the bid.

"$225," Elizabeth said calmly.

Randy looked at Elizabeth as a thought occurred to him. "Do you even have $225?" he demanded.

Elizabeth looked at her father and said cheekily, "I figured I'd just get it from you."

God doesn't have a budget. He has promised to supply all our needs (Philippians 4:19). Because this is His character, He doesn't budget His blessings to us. He has everything that we need, and He supplies everything we need out of His abundance. It's good to know that we do not have to have God's blessings auctioned off to us. He *gives* us what we need. We don't have to wish for things.

Discontent comes when we desire something we

don't have that we want, or when we are not happy with what God has provided. God wants us to have contented lives; to live at peace; to be joyful. When we trust God, we are content with what He gives us. He gives us everything we need to live the life He created for us to live. God is never stingy. What a wonderful Savior!

# Now Get to Sleep!

## Paul Muckley

*You make known to me the path of life;*
*you will fill me with joy in your presence,*
*with eternal pleasures at your right hand.*

Psalm 16:11 niv

What is it about bedtime that winds kids up?
I mean, really. . .the magical hour of 8 p.m.
arrives and my kids suddenly seem ready to watch a
feature-length film, eat a full meal, run the 400-meter
high hurdles, even construct a ninety-three-story skyscraper. And I'm not talking Legos here.

It's enough to drive a guy crazy. Much as I love my
kids, I need a little downtime, too. But as the kids get
older, my own quiet time gets rarer.

Early on, it seemed like the young 'uns went to bed
around seven, and sometimes clocked a good twelve
or thirteen hours before bursting forth—like a hail of
shotgun pellets—in the morning.

But somewhere around age four, they started rising
earlier. And they began fighting their bedtimes. And

Mom and Dad found themselves with much less free time than they'd enjoyed before. As the years go on, I'm feeling more and more like the weary baker in the old Dunkin' Donuts commercial—the guy slogging home after work and passing *himself* going back to the shop the next day.

Despite the tug-of-war, though, bedtime can have its good points. It's often the one time of day when my daughter opens up to discuss the more important issues of life.

I remember one conversation around her kindergarten year, starting off with the traditional opener, "Daaaaaad?"

"Yes, sweetheart?"

"What's heaven like?"

"Well, the Bible says it's a beautiful, happy place."

"Daaaaaad?"

"Yes, sweetie?"

"How do we get to heaven?"

"Well, we have to believe that Jesus died for our sins."

"Daaaaaad?"

"Yes, sweetie?"

"Why do skunks smell so bad?"

We call that a "short attention span."

But when kids desire something at bedtime, they can demonstrate an intense, laser-like mental focus. *Daddy, I want*. . .a drink of water, Vicks Vap-O-Rub (our kids *beg* for that stuff), one more book. You know, a short one like *War and Peace*.

One evening, after I tucked in our youngest, the just-turned-three-year-old lay in bed calling for another hug and kiss. Oh, and a snack. Oh, and his blanket.

Ultimately, I went to his room and told him I would bring him his blanket and some cereal. But, I insisted, "Until I get back, I want you to lie quietly and try to go to sleep."

He didn't argue. He just turned his big brown eyes my way and whispered a true toddler confession: "I'll be thinking about what you're bringing me."

Sometimes, you just have to laugh.

And sometimes God uses those humorous moments to unveil much larger truths.

It struck me that I, too, have a Father who's bringing me some good things. And until I "fall asleep" (the old Bible phrase for *die*), I can think about what God is going to give me—life without end, joy in His presence, eternal pleasures at His right hand.

And who knows? Maybe those pleasures will include a favorite blanket and the occasional snack of Cinnamon Toast Crunch.

# Papa Bear's in
# Good Hands

## Glenn A. Hascall

*You are my hiding place; you will protect me from
trouble and surround me with songs of deliverance.*
Psalm 32:7 niv

I'd planned in detail what I was going to say to the first
boy that thought dating my daughter was a good idea.
There would be some vague concept of personal risk, a
few meaningful glares, and if I played my cards right, the
boy would run away with a suitable amount of long-term
quivering.

Knowing my mind bent in this direction, my wife
engaged in covert operations that defused my interrogation-
style confrontation. She met him first. I think everyone
involved was relieved.

Gone are the fatherly dreams of a dating contract with
the young man specifying rules of behavior and decorum.
Gone, too, is the notion that I'd need to grunt ominously
instead of speaking cordially to the young man.

If I'd followed through on my original plan, I might

well have resembled a mountain man who's been left alone for years and suffered from an advanced case of rabies or a rather brutal toothache.

You can imagine my surprise when my daughter said, "You know, Daddy, my boyfriend really likes you."

Likes me? Did I want him to like me? I tried to be guarded and menacing. Somehow my "Grizzly" impression came across as "Teddy," and I was found to be likable.

Weird.

My daughter's beau likes our entire family. He loves to spend time with us. He expresses protective qualities toward my daughter that remind me of an aforementioned Papa Bear. They read God's Word together daily.

Is it possible I have forgotten what it was like to be young and in love? Honestly, this mirrored my own dating experience with my wife. There was nothing I wanted more than to protect and honor her.

My job has been to shield Alyssa to the best of my ability, but it won't be much longer before I will not be the one primarily responsible for my daughter. Each day is not only a step toward independence for her, but also a protective step back for me. Some days I struggle with this concept.

I still want to think of her as a little girl who held my hand while I read to her, the fourth-grader who needed someone to stand up for her, the one who wondered at times where she fit in and if others would accept her for who she is. With all those thoughts swirling in my head, I remember that we've always worked to make our home a refuge for our kids when life is hard. I think God planned it that way.

Alyssa may remember the refuge we offered in years to come, but right now she's preparing for a solo flight, and there will come a time when I can't and won't go with her. It's a moment we've been preparing for all her life. Even so, I expect this transition is going to be difficult for this likable grizzly bear.

The greatest comfort I have is in knowing God never backs away from the role of protector and provider. We never stop needing Him, and He never stops loving us even when this father thinks he knows best.

# RECOGNIZING THE PROBLEM

CONOVER SWOFFORD

*"'God, be merciful to me a sinner!'"*
LUKE 18:13 NKJV

Peter was alone at home with his daughters, three-year-old Macy and five-year-old Megan. Macy was in a misbehaving mood. No matter what Peter said or how he corrected her, Macy continued to misbehave. Finally, Peter put Macy into time-out and sat her on a chair. That didn't work, because Macy refused to stay on the chair. As Peter picked her up and put her back onto the chair for the third time, he said, exasperated, "What is your problem?"

Megan answered him, "I think you're her problem, Dad."

That surprised Peter. Despite Megan's statement, he was certain he didn't have a problem.

It's hard for us to realize that sometimes someone may think that we're their problem. We hardly ever perceive ourselves as being the problem. We don't want to think that any problem is our fault or that we've caused any problem. But the truth is, it's entirely possible for us to live our entire lives with a problem. . .a wrong perspective, an incorrect belief—and be totally oblivious to the problem. Luke 18:10–14 tells the story of two men, both of them had a problem, and one of the men was clueless about his problem.

One man, a Pharisee, was a leader in his community. He took pride in his position. He went to the Temple not to pray, but to tell God what a great guy he was. His focus was all on himself, not God. You'd think a guy like that would at least give God credit for making him so "great."

The other man, a tax collector, was despised in the community, mostly because he collected taxes from the people for the Romans. Nobody wanted to be his friend. He went to the Temple because he recognized that he *knew* he was unrighteous before God and he wanted to correct it. He asked God for mercy.

We should not strive to be like the Pharisee, unaware that our problem is us. We don't want our focus to be on how terrific we think we are. If we are like that, people around us will recognize our problem, even if we don't.

God wants us to humble ourselves before Him. How wonderful to know that even when we cannot properly express our thoughts, feelings, or wishes, God knows exactly what we're trying to say. When our hearts are too anguished or overwhelmed for us to express ourselves coherently, the Holy Spirit gently and kindly interprets our prayers for us. After all, He knows us better than we know ourselves.

When we take our faulty selves and humbly before God's throne of grace say, "Please be merciful to me," God answers that prayer with a "yes" every time.

# DAD-OLOGY 101: MAKING MEMORIES

*Sometimes the poorest man leaves
his children the richest inheritance.*
RUTH E. RENKEL

# LET THEM COME

JAMES LOW

*People were bringing little children to*
*Jesus for him to place his hands on them,*
*but the disciples rebuked them. When Jesus saw this,*
*he was indignant. He said to them,*
*"Let the little children come to me, and do not hinder*
*them, for the kingdom of God belongs to such as these."*

MARK 10:13–14 NIV

Dave and I have always been friends. He was born the day after I was. Our parents met in the hospital. They discovered they were neighbors and made it a point to get us together. It's been said that our timely births gave birth to our friendship. This is reflected in the fact that we celebrated every childhood birthday party together. During our younger years we were inseparable. We'd spend the night at each other's houses, go to summer camps together, and even go on each other's family vacations.

We grew up in a quiet suburban neighborhood set in the shadow of one of America's famous historic cities.

Our parents would regularly take us downtown to the zoo, to museums, to eat, and to watch baseball games (our favorite!). Dave's dad was a bigwig at his engineering company. We spent a good deal of time at his offices which happened to be located downtown. When I say "his engineering company" I'm not joking. He was an owner of the company and acted as chief executive officer. He also owned the building that housed his company's offices.

I only mention all of this because Dave's dad would take Dave, his younger brother, and me to visit his office before our other scheduled city activities. While Dave's dad attended to important last-minute work or finished up a meeting, we were given key cards and let loose. We'd invade the snack room then run amok playing hide-and-seek. On more than one occasion we encountered an employee working late to meet some deadline. They never said it, but you could tell they weren't thrilled with having to endure our intrusions.

I've realized a lot looking back on these moments. Not only did everyone understand that we weren't to be treated like we were "in the way," but also, Dave's dad never kept us at arm's length. If we needed him for anything at any time, all we had to do was walk in and ask him. It wasn't until much later that I realized how out of the ordinary this was. Dave's dad was the head of a high profile company. Businessmen from all over had to schedule appointments and make time for meetings with him, but not only did he make time for us kids, he made himself available to us even in the midst of his all-important work.

Dave's dad's example reminds us of the time when Jesus tells the disciples not to hinder the children from coming to Him. The disciples were learning that Jesus was THE "CEO" but they erred in thinking He was too important and busy to waste time with children. What about us? Being a dad is a busy full-time job wrought with responsibility. Even in trying to be the best dads we can, we need to ask ourselves, "Do our children feel they're just in the way, or do they know that they are our priority?"

# So Many Books, So Little Sleep

## Gayle Lintz

*"Which of you, if your son asks for bread,*
*will give him a stone?"*
Matthew 7:9 niv

My dad loved to read. Each Sunday afternoon, he would read the newspaper's "funnies" aloud to us. There were always books in our home and magazines like *Saturday Evening Post*, *Time*, *Life*, and *Reader's Digest*. Dad kept a stack of books, fiction and nonfiction, on his bedside table. My sister and I became readers, too.

When I was in high school, we were studying the Civil War just as a movie studio was reissuing the movie *Gone with the Wind*. I thought the Pulitzer prize-winning novel might be a good read, and I located a copy. Sixty-three chapters. If I read one or two chapters every evening, I could finish in a month or two, and that wouldn't be too much to add to my regular schoolwork.

The first evening, I read a chapter. The story was compelling, and I was reluctant to put the book down after chapter one. The next night, I got right to work on homework, finished it quickly, and picked up the book again and began chapter two. I was hooked. I read and read. The war began. There was a barbecue, weddings, a death, a birth. I raced through chapter after chapter. The plot expanded with more characters, more issues, more problems.

I heard my sister preparing for bed. I stayed in my room and read. Later, I heard my parents, turning off the television, walking down the hallway to their bedroom. I kept reading. Things were growing worse for the people of the South, the citizens of Atlanta. General Sherman was determined to destroy the Confederacy, laying waste to the land.

I knew I should be sleeping, but I couldn't stop. Atlanta was on fire, every character was in danger. How would Scarlet O'Hara get the people for whom she was responsible, back to her family home—to Tara?

At about 2 a.m., I heard a soft knock on my bedroom door. Dad poked in his head. "It's late" he said. "You should get to sleep."

I held up the book. "The Yankees are coming," I said.

"Oh," he said, nodding, and he shut the door and went back down the hall.

I read for a while longer, into chapter twenty-four, at a point where all the tension of the previous chapters reached a climax. Exhausted, I put down the book and slept.

I appreciated that my dad let me keep on reading,

*way, way* past my bedtime. I suppose he realized that, if I was so involved in the story, stopping in the middle of such suspense wasn't going to get me to sleep. I appreciate more, as a parent, the delicate balance between not only setting rules and guidelines but also knowing when to be rigid and when to be flexible. Loving parents evaluate a situation and make a decision based on what a particular child needs at a particular place and time. Thanks, Dad.

# Fish Oil—
# the Nectar of Life

## Glenn A. Hascall

*"Come, follow me," Jesus said,*
*"and I will send you out to fish for people."*
### Matthew 4:19 niv

I'm a long-time fisher of fish. That means I clean the fish and cook them outside. I have to change clothes. I need a breath mint. My wife is not a big fan.

However, my daughter has always had an incredible curiosity about the critters I have brought home on a stringer. Let's go back a few years.

"Whatcha doin', Daddy?" She stares at the bucket.

"I'm cleaning fish," I reply.

"Are they dirty?"

"No. I'm getting them ready to eat."

"I don't wanna eat them like this. They are dipscusting."

"You mean disgusting."

"That's what I said."

"Oh."

"I don't wanna watch."

"You can go inside if you want."

"You know, Daddy, this is really gross. Can that fish see me?" She hands me another fish and grins. She doesn't leave.

Alyssa developed a taste for fish at an early age. On the advice of a nutritionist we gave her fish oil as a baby. It was supposed to improve her health and give her extra brainpower. Because she was our first child, we wanted to do everything perfectly and were scared to death we were failing. Somehow fish oil was supposed to develop perfect children.

Once when I was getting my daughter ready for preschool I conducted a quick review of the pantry and chose to make salmon patties for my lunch at work.

"Hey Daddy," she began, "can I have some salmon?"

"Sure," I replied, emptying the contents of the can into a bowl.

I allowed the stove to warm up while I found my shoes.

"This is really good," she called from the kitchen.

I mumbled as I tried to decide between athletic shoes or some slip-ons. When I got back to the kitchen Alyssa said, "Got any more?"

So much for lunch.

Today most of Alyssa's favorite foods include fish. She considers fish oil pills chewable. Her friends are left queasy when they take her up on the suggestion and sample her pills. I believe the experience may be similar to kissing a trout.

This observation led me to consider what role fish might play in common fairy tales: *The Fish Princess, A Cinderella Trout Story, Snow Whitefish off the Seven Wharfs,* or *Goldencod and the Three Bass.*

I'm not aware of many individuals who love fish as much as Alyssa does, but her response has caused me to think about how I interact with my children.

God wants me to be faithful in the act of being a daddy. That may require that I accept the unique textures of my children in the same way Alyssa adores fish. My kids should always feel acceptance and love from me. I set boundaries and there are consequences for wrong choices, but my love doesn't stop just because my children have personalities that are different than mine. I will keep fishing for their hearts.

Every moment I spend with my kids offers potential for lifelong memories. That could be at a singing competition, a baseball game, or the moment guests chew on a fish oil pill at the advice of a teenage girl who thinks it's the nectar of life.

Dream on, sweet princess.

# GET YOUR HANDS DIRTY

## PAUL MUCKLEY

*In your relationships with one another,*
*have the same mindset as Christ Jesus:*
*Who, being in very nature God, did not consider*
*equality with God something to be used to his*
*own advantage; rather, he made himself nothing*
*by taking the very nature of a servant, being*
*made in human likeness. . . . He humbled himself.*
PHILIPPIANS 2:5–8 NIV

If you're going to be a good dad, you'll have to get your hands dirty.

In the literal sense, you'll handle spit-up and diaper-doo by the semi-truckload. You'll scrape cracker and cheese residue off your shirt sleeve and pant leg—which you'll only notice *after* you've arrived at the office. And you'll have greasy fingers and bloody knuckles as you fix that uncooperative bicycle chain for the umpteenth time.

But I'm thinking more abstractly—"get your hands dirty" as in "lower yourself to your kids' level."

If you're going to be a good dad, you'll have to get down on your kids' level to play:

- You'll be a courteous guest at your daughter's tea parties.
- You'll reacquaint yourself with Crayola crayons—especially periwinkle and burnt sienna.
- You'll spend hours working your way through a 96-page Lego kit manual.
- You'll actually dress a Barbie doll.

And, if you're going to be a good dad, you'll have to condescend to your kids' intellectual level:

- You'll sing about twinkling stars, little lambs, and itsy-bitsy (or possibly "eensy-weensy") spiders.
- You'll read *The Very Hungry Caterpillar* at least 768 times. . .in a week.
- You'll watch episode after episode of *Scooby Doo*—and wonder just why you enjoyed it so much as a kid.
- You'll "laugh" at their "jokes," such as, "Why did the dog bark? Because he's a dog! Ha ha! Ha ha! Ha ha ha!"

And, finally, if you're going to be a good dad, you'll experience *all* the various aspects of life at your kids' level:

- You'll occasionally, in a pinch, wear a *Little Mermaid* or *Transformers* Band-Aid.

- You'll occasionally, in an emergency, brush with Barney Bubble-Fruity Toothpaste.
- You'll occasionally, at your kids' request, carry a plastic action figure or stuffed animal to work—and display it proudly on your desk.
- You'll tell everyone around you how really terrific your kids are.

So why would a grown man get into "kid stuff"? For the same reason God became Man. It's all about love.

You love your kids; God loves His kids. You'll get down to your kids' level; He'll get down to yours.

Dirty hands for everyone!

# "Father" Not "Friend"

## James Low

*No discipline seems pleasant at the time, but painful.*
*Later on, however, it produces a harvest of righteousness*
*and peace for those who have been trained by it.*
Hebrews 12:11 niv

Fathers today consistently confess to struggling with being "the bad guy" as opposed to "the buddy" when it comes to raising their kids. This is particularly true during the teenage years when the teenagers' increased independence and know-it-all attitudes create a rift between father and child. All too often the dad feels that enforcing any type of discipline will only cause to further the distance between him and his kids, so he resorts to being his kids' "friend" instead of their "father."

Thankfully my dad did not have this problem. He frequently enforced his guiding decisions and exercised discipline. Unfortunately this often ran completely contrary to what I desired and infringed upon my freedom. As an adolescent I unfairly accused him of being a "dictator" instead of a dad, and remember retorting to his decisions and discipline with "I wish you were more like so-and-so's dad, he lets us do whatever we want." My dad would only reply "Well, I wish I could be, but I'm your father, not your friend."

I now know how much it must have pained my dad to hear me say such things and treat him as I did, but he endured it knowing that my temporary "unpleasantness" was necessary for me to grow and mature. Looking back I have no doubt that it was my dad's willingness to "be the bad guy" instead of my "buddy" that helped cultivate a healthy relationship based on love, respect, and appreciation between the two of us as I officially entered adulthood. Not only this, but because of it I recognized my own need for discipline as well as the harvest of blessing it has produced in my own life.

It won't be easy, for our children or for us, but as fathers we need to be brave enough to be just that—fathers instead of friends.

# Daddy Day Care

## Paul Muckley

*For lack of guidance a nation falls,*
*but victory is won through many advisers.*
### Proverbs 11:14 niv

It was just like the 2003 Eddie Murphy comedy *Daddy Day Care.*

Well, not *exactly* like it. I hadn't just been laid off and started a child-care business. And I didn't have fourteen kids and various animals roaming around my home. And I wasn't under investigation by Children's Services.

But it was close enough. All by my little lonesome, I was watching our two kids—five-year-old daughter, three-year-old son—while my wife disappeared for a long weekend. It was some kind of Christian women's conference, but really—what kind of "Christian women" leave their kids under dads' supervision for three days?

Actually, I think I'm pretty responsible. Pretty capable. Even pretty nice-looking, though that's not important now. And I had organized a weekend of fatherly fun and frolic that historians would study for centuries to come.

I'd taken Friday afternoon off work, with plans to attend a matinee showing of the Disney/Pixar film *Cars*. We'd be hanging with Lightning, Mater, and the crew for a couple of hours—and I knew a pre-movie snack was a good idea. Otherwise, I might have to cash out the kids' college fund to buy food at the theater.

While eating a very healthy, appropriate, dad-approved snack, though, my daughter looked quizzically at her apple and asked, "What's this?" We both squinted at the small, hard, white thingy sticking out of the fruit's skin.

*Oh no—it's one of her teeth!*

Jagged on the bottom edge. . .a little blood on her gums. . .did she break it off? Did she need surgery? Was she going to make it through the weekend? What does a responsible, capable, nice-looking dad do now?

I gathered my wits and called our family medical consultant—the helpful, older nurse who lives a quarter-mile up the road.

*Uh-oh. . .she isn't home.*

Okay then, maybe I'll check with our longtime family dentist instead.

*Friday afternoon. . .they aren't answering either.*

Man, I'm sure he could have helped. . .I mean, he's been seeing me since I had baby teeth!

*Wait—baby teeth? Hmmmm. . .*

When all else fails, every responsible, capable, forty-year-old guy knows exactly who to call.

"Hello, Mom?"

When I explained her granddaughter's condition and her son's consternation, Mom laughed. "Oh Paul," she said, "kids just lose teeth at this age."

It was nice of her not to add, "Silly!"

Now, in my defense, let it be said that my daughter had never once mentioned that any tooth was loose. Nor had she ever vocalized plans for any money the tooth fairy might bring her. The sudden gap in her chompers surprised her as much as it did me.

Honestly, life throws plenty of confusing curveballs our way. And to sort things out, we need all the help we can get—from the Bible, our church, wife, friends, coworkers, FedEx guys, you name it. God puts people all around us to help us out. So let 'em!

And, by the way, thanks, Mom.

# TEENAGERS!

P. REGINALD LEGUME

*Prudence is a fountain of life to the prudent.*
PROVERBS 16:22 NIV

What can cause a man so much pain that his mind is tormented *almost daily* with unpleasant thoughts? In my case it boiled down to one simple word:

*Teenagers!*

I might as well just be honest. Before my little assignment, I did not care for teenagers. In my humble opinion, teenagers were—as a general rule—big, smelly, and did things with eggs and toilet paper I wanted to describe in intimate, vivid detail.[1]

But because God knows my heart, and because He is an all-knowing, loving heavenly Father, He decided to give me a special blessing. You guessed it! *He put me in charge of our church's teens.* Specifically the Youth Worship Team.

---

1. Unfortunately my editor would only allow me to use the word "inappropriate."

Needless to say, I was in over my head. But at least my church-brothers were supportive and encouraging.[2] It turns out the solution was really quite simple: Heavy medication! Ha, ha! Just kidding!

But I digress. Does your church have a Youth Worship Team?

It's an interesting experience to say the least. Have you ever given a group of playful, energetic teenagers expensive, professional microphones then plugged them into a powerful, state-of-the-art sound system?

Teens love to talk. But, oh my word, you haven't heard *anything* until you've given them the ability to converse at volume levels that can utterly blot out the sound of a full-blown, global, nuclear holocaust. Which, come to think of it, is pretty much what our worship sounded like.

But after a few months of "hanging with my peeps" as the hip, new generation of Christian young people like to say, something very strange began to occur. . .

I actually began to *like* the dirty, smelly, loud-mouthed, beady-eyed, fur-covered little weasels—and I'm not talking about the Board of Elders—I'm talking about the *students*!

Teens tell it like it is. I came to appreciate that quite a bit. Sure, they're not always the easiest folks to be around. But they're definitely a lot of fun. And when a teenager tells you he loves you, you know you can believe it. What a blessing!

_____

2. "That's not how you do it, you moron! Who put you in charge, anyway?"

# THE DAD POWERHOUSE 2: CONNECTING TO GOD

*Don't worry about what you do not understand. . . .*
*Worry about what you do understand in*
*the Bible but do not live by.*

CORRIE TEN BOOM

# Who Is That Guy?

## Paul Muckley

> *"The righteous will answer him,*
> *'Lord, when did we see you hungry and feed you,*
> *or thirsty and give you something to drink?*
> *When did we see you a stranger and invite you in,*
> *or needing clothes and clothe you?*
> *When did we see you sick or in prison and go*
> *to visit you?' The King will reply, 'Truly I tell you,*
> *whatever you did for one of the least of these*
> *brothers and sisters of mine, you did for me.'"*
>
> MATTHEW 25:37–40 NIV

Ever seen the game called Don't Break the Ice? Depending on the age of the kids playing, it might be better known as Don't Break My Face.

That's because those kids are actually swinging hammers.

Okay, so the hammers are small. And they're made of plastic. But my kids swung them with such ferocity that I often feared for my life.

If you're not familiar with Don't Break the Ice, where

have you been, man? It goes back to the late 1960s.

The game consists of a small, table-shaped platform into which you press about thirty white plastic cubes. The cubes measure roughly an inch on each side, though there's a larger piece—about the size of four cubes together—that fits in the center. On top of that larger piece sits a little, red plastic man who hunches over ever so slightly. Maybe he's ice fishing, or praying, or experiencing the effects of food poisoning. It's hard to say.

What I do know is that the rules of the game tell players to use their hammers to gently tap individual cubes down through the platform. One player knocks out a cube, then the next player tries to do the same, and so on. . .until at some point all the remaining cubes—and the little red man—fall through. That last player "breaks the ice" and loses the game.

But such intricacies are lost on two- to four-year-olds, for whom it's much more fun to simply whack away at the ice. Hey, if you can knock out every cube with *one* swing—and maybe send pieces skittering under the stove and refrigerator—it's an absolute laugh riot!

Just as funny in our family, though, was the identity of that little red man. Our toddler son was absolutely convinced it was "Jesus."

And why not? Though we have no record of Jesus ever getting food poisoning, He may well have fished (remember Peter and Andrew, James and John, the commercial fishermen-turned-followers of Jesus?). Without question, Jesus prayed. And He has a way of showing up in some rather unexpected places—in the hospital, in jail, in a used clothing distribution center, in a soup line.

No, really.

That's the whole point of Jesus' "sheep and goats" parable in Matthew 25. One way He'll identify His true followers is by how they treated the less-well-off around them, because "'whatever you did for one of the least of these brothers and sisters of mine, you did for me.'"

So who is that guy? Well, of course, it's Jesus!

# A Parable about Radish Seeds

## Paul M. Miller

*"Still other seed fell on good soil, where it produced a crop—a hundred, sixty or thirty times what was sown. Whoever has ears, let them hear."*

Matthew 13:8–9 NIV

Radishes have always been daughter Lisa's favorite seed to plant in the vegetable garden. String beans were generally our second favorite veggie seed. They were slower, but the crooked sprout was always fun to see.

For some reason we didn't seem to have luck with peas, but that was okay, because we didn't enjoy them as much as we did green beans and radishes.

While some neighbors bought already-growing vegetable plants from the nursery, whenever possible we went the seed route. Lisa enjoyed going over to Ace Hardware and studying all the colorful packets on the display racks. She'd weigh the benefits of each—mostly growing time. But of course, she'd inevitably select radishes—they were fast growers.

Her grandfather taught her how to plant seeds in a straight row. He'd pound a little stake on one side of the garden plot and another on the opposite side. Then he'd tie a string between the two stakes. When the seeds were safely patted into the groove he'd drawn with his finger, he'd stick the packet on one of the stakes and give the row a good dousing with his watering can. So did Lisa.

Sure as anything, the next morning after planting, Lisa was on her knees looking for a tell-tale radish sprout. She could hardly wait for the first flat, green leaf to pop up.

Stepping off the school bus in the afternoons, she'd make a dash to the backyard and her row of radish seeds. Any little hindrance like a tree twig was quickly removed. Nothing was allowed to impede the growth of her veggies.

One Saturday afternoon I found Lisa lying flat on her stomach with her eyes a couple of millimeters from the dirt. "Any sign of life?" I called out.

Rather discouraged, she answered with a deeply sighed, "No."

The next day after school, Lisa came running into the house all excited with a *Weekly Reader* story about talking to plants for better growth.

"Isn't this wonderful!" Lisa enthused. "I'm going try it!"

Then, with ulterior motive, I suggested, "How about reading some scripture to them? The Bible has a lot to say about seeds."

"What shall I read?"

"You might start with Matthew 13—Jesus' parable about a farmer."

The next night at dinner, Lisa updated the family on her radish growth experiment. "I did like Daddy suggested. . .I read the Bible to my radish seeds."

"Which part?" her mother asked.

"This part," Lisa responded, reaching for a Bible on the buffet. Then she read about the farmer who planted seeds; some came up and produced a crop, others didn't. With a broad smile my daughter read, " 'Other seed fell on good soil, where it produced a crop—a hundred, sixty or thirty times what was sown.' That's what my radishes will do!"

And "do it," they did. Two weeks later, after a bountiful harvest, radish-stuffed Tim was heard to remark, "Whatever you do, Lisa, please don't read the Bible to Dad's zucchinis."

# Twenty-First-Century Communication Is Old School

## Glenn A. Hascall

*"Every word of God is flawless."*
**Proverbs 30:5 niv**

H EY, DAD, COULD YOU MAKE ME BREAKFAST?" This is a standard question from my daughter, Alyssa, most Saturday mornings.

"SURE, WHAT WOULD YOU LIKE?"

"SURPRISE ME."

I often wonder if guacamole dip on a bagel covered in candy sprinkles would be a surprise, but I usually go with what I know she likes. No use wasting a good bagel.

The most interesting part of our exchange is that neither of us has uttered a single word to the other. I haven't even seen her. The correspondence was all completed by text messages.

There was a time when the equivalent of text messaging was either a telegram or Morse code. This type of text messaging was usually reserved for emergencies. Does a breakfast order qualify as a crisis?

This is not my preferred method of talking to my daughter, but for some reason she enjoys texting me from her room so she can rest a little longer while breakfast smells waft throughout our home.

The first time she sent me a text was to ask if I would come pick her up from school. At the time I had a phone that required me to hit one number at least three times to get a single letter then another number two times for the next. It seems like I had to hit 487,302 buttons just to post, "OK. I'LL BE RIGHT THERE."

After giving up, I got in my vehicle and went to pick her up. She called asking, "Where are you, Daddy? I was waiting for a text."

With an incredible sense of calm I replied, "Well, I could either text you or pick you up. Do you have a preference?"

I'm not always thrilled with the technological advances that seem to detract from face-to-face conversations. I still struggle with attempting a conversation with my daughter that's interrupted by texts from her friends.

Owning up to being a closet curmudgeon is hard to admit, but in the spirit of full disclosure I needed to confess to my personal defect. Yes, I do feel better.

My daughter understands this struggle, yet she persists in texting me. I think she considers it a technological intervention program.

If this were the only way she wanted to talk to me,

I might be more concerned. However, once I got a phone with a keyboard, my acceptance of this form of communication improved (especially when my daughter is on a school trip or visiting friends).

No matter how she wants to communicate, the good news is she still likes to talk to me. Not bad for a teenager.

There are times when she'll text, "I JUST HAD A RANDOM URGE TO TELL YOU I LOVE YOU, DADDY." Yeah, that's a keeper, if I could only figure out how to find it again. Other times she will say, "WHY DO BOYS HAVE TO BE SO STUPID?" I'm not sure she really expects me to have an answer.

Maybe I shouldn't struggle so much. God's Word is the first text message, and I endeavor to review His message daily. His biblical communication is always a keeper. The best news is, I don't have to text in order to respond.

# HISTORY-MAKING

PAUL MUCKLEY

> *"My Father, if it is possible,*
> *may this cup be taken from me.*
> *Yet not as I will, but as you will."*
> MATTHEW 26:39 NIV

Some events are so historic, you never forget them:

The day humans first walked on the moon.

The night the US elected its first black president.

The weekend you accompanied your son on his first Cub Scout campout.

My experience with the latter featured all the typical stuff: rustic setting in the woods. . .toilet facilities of the non-flushing variety. . .wild-eyed boys dancing around a fire, incinerating marshmallows on long sticks.

I hoped to enjoy some of the sounds of nature: the song of the crested warbler, the chirp of the tufted titmouse, maybe the chatter of the gray squirrel. But since the temperature was only thirty-five degrees and the humidity approximately 400 percent, the wildlife had wisely gone indoors for the night. I think I saw their bus parked outside the local Holiday Inn.

That's not to say it was a silent night. The eighteen creatures packed into a shelter the size of my bedroom (believe me, I don't live in a palace) created quite enough noise, thank you. Human though we all were, there were several recognizable subspecies:

1) the Crested Whiner: Occasionally sang its irritating song, but thankfully proved to be scarce.
2) the Tufted Tootmouse: Expect to hear its call whenever juveniles of the species congregate. Typically followed by the cry of Laughing Guy-enas.
3) the Graying Snorel: These critters (the half-dozen thirty- and forty-something men chaperoning) raised quite a racket through the night. A trained ear could distinguish the various snorels present: the Rumbling Snorel, the Snorting Snorel, and the Chainsawing Snorel.

I am pleased to announce that I made no embarrassing, involuntary noises in my sleep. That's because I never fell asleep that night.

While I generally don't rest well on overly-soft mattresses, my sleeping-bag-on-a-picnic-table bed was a bit firm for my taste. The little wood burner in the corner of the pavilion pumped out enough heat to make a nearby thermometer read eighty-six degrees—though beyond a radius of approximately fifteen inches the temperature quickly dropped back to the just-above-frostbite level of my toes. For hour upon sleepless hour, I found myself praying the final prayer of the Bible: "Come quickly, Lord Jesus."

What I'm about to say proves how easy my life has been—but without exaggeration, this was the most physically uncomfortable experience of my forty-five years. The following day, easing my aching, shivering body into a tub of hot water, I vowed, "Never again."

There's another side to the campout story though: My son loved it.

# WE COULD HAVE
# NAMED HIM STORM

GLENN A. HASCALL

*Jesus said, "Let the little children come to me,
and do not hinder them, for the kingdom
of heaven belongs to such as these."*

MATTHEW 19:14 NIV

When my son was born, he was front-page news. Some births seem almost normal. Don't get me wrong, every birth is miraculous and wonderful, but some just seem to go off without a hitch. Not so with Ryan.

He started his journey toward birth with implantation issues that caused doctors to think we were losing him. We didn't. He grew so large that he ultimately caused my wife to collapse when he pressed on a certain nerve. Did he think that was funny?

On the day of his birth I had all the bags ready to go. Contractions were sporadic, so we waited. By late afternoon I made the decision to head to the maternity ward. The sky was a peculiar color that I've since come to think of as a predictor of doom. A couple of blocks away from our home we heard the tornado sirens blare, rain began to fall, and softball-sized hail pulverized our vehicle.

We pulled over and waited for the storm to stop, but the atmospheric assault broke windows, totaled our car, and stopped Nancy's labor.

A week later a reporter showed up and took some pictures. We recounted the story in as much detail as they wanted. They printed the results.

I don't think I'm the only one to ever wonder how we dads can be entrusted to care for our children. We are the guys who can't remember to lower the toilet seat, shut the garage door, or drop off the electric bill. We forget anniversaries, birthdays, and school plays. We rarely get everything on a grocery list, but somehow manage to bring home every shiny thing that caught our eye. Yet, when a son or daughter is placed in our arms, we begin to understand that we were created for more than video games, bowling nights, and pizza.

Our children need us, and they look to us to be their role model. I'm proof positive we won't get it right all the time, but we can begin to recognize the need to view daddy-hood as more than a college certification class.

More than a dozen years have passed since my son came through a storm and brought new life into our family. He hates to take out the trash, loathes making his bed, resists showers, wants to stay up past his bedtime, and discourages the celebration of taco night. He's also generous, compassionate, honest, kind, and less pesky around his sister than hornets at a family picnic.

My son didn't have a typical birth, but his story helps me remember to make sure my car insurance is current, to pay closer attention to the weather, and to pass along the details of God's love because as close as I want to be to my son, there is One with whom I want him to be closer.

# THE GOOD NEW DAYS

### DAVID MCLAUGHLAN

*Jesus did many other things as well.*
*If every one of them were written down,*
*I suppose that even the whole world would not*
*have room for the books that would be written.*

JOHN 21:25 NIV

I just got a text message from my twenty-nine-year-old daughter Stacey. It read, "DAD-DAD-DAD-DAD-DAD! I JUST BOUGHT 'WATERSHIP DOWN' ON DVD!!!!!! J."

Well, I could tell she was excited. Honestly, though, I couldn't understand *why*.

Then I remembered that this is Stacey. If there's one thing Stacey likes above everything else it is a hearkening back to the "good old days" of her childhood. Though she is married with a husband and family of her own, she has spent quite a bit of money buying toys and books that remind her of her childhood.

I suppose it's a compliment to her mother and I. But. . .*Watership Down*? I knew the story. It was about a bunch of rabbits searching for a safe place to live. Didn't

Art Garfunkel sing the theme song?

The thing was, I didn't think I had ever watched it with Stacey.

So, I replied in a way that would sound enthusiastic, without actually having committed myself to anything. I messaged back, "YAYYYYY! ENJOY! X." ("X", by the way, is our affectionate father-to-daughter kiss via text).

"OHHH! I WILL. X," she replied

Well. . .I could have just let it go. But those good old days were important to me, too, and I didn't like feeling I had mislaid one. So, I nervously texted, "DID WE WATCH THAT WAY BACK WHEN? X."

Her immediate reply simply said, "OHHH, DAD!!!"

You may have noticed. No kiss. I felt like a bad, bad dad!

Then my cell buzzed again.

"IT MUST BE DIFFICULT," she messaged, "TO REMEMBER PARTICULAR GOOD TIMES. AFTER ALL, YOU GAVE US SO MANY!" And this message ended, "J."

I was delighted! Mostly because she had resisted the temptation to insert the words, "AT YOUR AGE" at the end of the text.

We did have good times. Lots of them! And, okay, as the father of a twenty-nine-year-old, I'm maybe not young enough anymore to remember them all.

The Gospels were written decades after the life of Christ, perhaps by old men, perhaps by young men retelling the stories of old men. (I'm not that old. . . honest!)

Maybe they remembered the most dramatic tales. John himself wrote that not all the books in the world could record the things Jesus did (John 21:25). Though we don't know these stories, I am sure they warmed the hearts of those who heard them. They would have remembered them and told others, helping to spread the truth about salvation.

Jesus is still working in our lives. If we walk beside Him, we are sure to have wonderful experiences. Let's be sure and tell others about these experiences, in case we should forget the occasional miracle in among all the other "good old days" He sends us.

# THE DOGWOOD TREE

GAYLE LINTZ

*And they were calling to one another:*
*"Holy, holy, holy is the LORD Almighty;*
*the whole earth is full of his glory."*
ISAIAH 6:3 NIV

My dad was a wonderful yardman. I remember him mowing and edging the lawn each week, from spring into early fall. We had a garden with radishes, carrots, green onions, and tomatoes. Some things flourished, like the pecan tree which still grows in the yard today. Other plants came and went, like a trio of small maples that lived for a while, then drooped and never became healthy again.

Inspired by a springtime trip to East Texas, Dad bought a dogwood tree, planning to enjoy its lovely blossoms each March. Problem was, here in Central Texas, the soil and climate are not great for dogwoods. But he made the commitment to enrich the dirt, fertilize, and carefully tend his little baby tree to adulthood—to be as strong and beautiful as possible.

Every spring we got new outfits for Easter Sunday. And each year, we arranged ourselves for outdoor photos. Often, the dogwood tree would be in bloom, and it seemed the perfect place to take pictures. So there are photos of me and my sister, smiling in the spring sunshine, standing *behind* the blooming dogwood tree. Or posed *beside* the dogwood and its blossoms. There are certainly no pictures of us standing in *front* of the tree. What would be the point in that? You wouldn't be able to see the glorious flowers!

Winters are relatively mild in Central Texas. We'll have a freeze once or twice each year. Sometimes the temperature will dip into the teens. But daffodils bloom in February, and the average last freeze day is March 15. One year, the dogwood began to bud a little early. Our weather can be erratic, and the local meteorologist forecast a late freeze. That evening, Dad watched the weather reports with despair, fearing the dogwood's little green buds would be damaged by the unfortunate cold snap. The year's flowers were in danger.

When I woke up the next morning, I opened my blinds to a most unusual sight. The dogwood tree, just outside my window, was glowing softly in the dawn. An extension cord ran across the back yard and wound up the dogwood tree's trunk, powering a string of Christmas lights. Each glowing bulb was clipped on a branch right next to a bud. (Note to the youngsters: Years ago, those kinds of bulbs got hot enough to burn fingers.)

Dad's unorthodox plan worked. The buds were safe.

They opened on time, and we had beautiful dogwood flowers. You can see them clearly in that year's Easter photograph of me and my sister, as we are seated *beneath* the tree.

The earth is indeed full of God's glory. We see it in the sunshine and the rain, the snow and the stars. We see it in red tomatoes and orange carrots. We see it in the strong trunks of pecan trees and the fragile flowers of the dogwood. Great is our God.

# CONTRIBUTORS

**Glenn A. Hascall** is an accomplished writer with credits in more than fifty books, including titles from Thomas Nelson, Bethany House, and Regal. His articles have appeared in numerous publications including the *Wall Street Journal*. He's also an award-winning broadcaster, lending his voice to national radio and television networks.

**Gayle Lintz** has written preschool teaching materials for Lifeway Christian Resources for several years and has been published in various Christian devotional periodicals. Gayle lives with her husband in Waco, Texas, where they are members of Calvary Baptist Church. They have two married sons who live in Fort Worth, Texas, and Brooklyn, New York.

**James Low** is finishing up a Masters of Divinity program at Gordon-Conwell Theological Seminary. He and his wife recently relocated to Tallahassee to serve in ministry. James has worked as a writer, providing scripts and screenplays for Christian production companies.

**David McLaughlan** lives in Scotland with his wife, Julie, and a whole clan of their children. When he decided to stop writing about any old thing and focus on faith and God, he expected his career to disappear without a trace. But it didn't! That makes his heart sing!

**Paul M. Miller** lives on Whidbey Island in Washington state. He's a retired writer/editor, and father of two grown children—Lisa and Tim. Paul's commitment to Christ, His church, and outreach are apparent in his productions of church-centered dinner theater programs. He's the author of drama handbooks and plays, as well as inspirational and humor books. His life scripture is Ephesians 4:23–24.

**Paul Muckley** serves as senior editor for nonfiction at Barbour Publishing. Under the pseudonym Paul Kent, he has written several books of Bible trivia. Paul enjoys history, railroads, and bicycling; mushrooms are definitely not among his favorite things. He and his wife, Laurie, have adopted three children and live in eastern Ohio.

**P. Reginald Legume** is a world famous, full-time, professional author, except on Sunday morning when he is involved in a tiny little church plant which has rendered him completely insane resulting in the devotions you will find in this book.

**Conover Swofford** lives in Columbus, Georgia. A freelance writer for over twenty-five years, Conover enjoys reading and participates in many of her church's community activities.

# Scripture Index

# OLD TESTAMENT

Genesis

    2:15. . . . . . . . . . . . . . . . . . . . . . . . . . . . . . . . . . . . . . 22
    3:9. . . . . . . . . . . . . . . . . . . . . . . . . . . . . . . . . . . . . . . 49
    22:1–2. . . . . . . . . . . . . . . . . . . . . . . . . . . . . . . . . . . 129

Exodus

    20:5–6. . . . . . . . . . . . . . . . . . . . . . . . . . . . . . . . . . 162
    20:12. . . . . . . . . . . . . . . . . . . . . . . . . . . . . 18, 109

Deuteronomy

    6:6–7. . . . . . . . . . . . . . . . . . . . . . . . . . . . . . . . . . . . 156

Joshua

    1:9. . . . . . . . . . . . . . . . . . . . . . . . . . . . . . . . . . . . . . . 90

2 Samuel

    11:1. . . . . . . . . . . . . . . . . . . . . . . . . . . . . . . . . . . . . . 99

Job

    1:5. . . . . . . . . . . . . . . . . . . . . . . . . . . . . . . . . . . . . . 168
    41:1. . . . . . . . . . . . . . . . . . . . . . . . . . . . . . . . . . . . . 148
    41:11. . . . . . . . . . . . . . . . . . . . . . . . . . . . . . . . . . . . 138

Psalms

    16:11. . . . . . . . . . . . . . . . . . . . . . . . . . . . . . . . . . . . 194
    27:7. . . . . . . . . . . . . . . . . . . . . . . . . . . . . . . . . . . . . . 68
    32:7. . . . . . . . . . . . . . . . . . . . . . . . . . . . . . . . . . . . 197

119:105. . . . . . . . . . . . . . . . . . . . . . . . . . . . . . 74
139:7–8. . . . . . . . . . . . . . . . . . . . . . . . . . . . . 46
147:4–5. . . . . . . . . . . . . . . . . . . . . . . . . . . . . 52
149:1. . . . . . . . . . . . . . . . . . . . . . . . . . . . . . 115

Proverbs

3:5. . . . . . . . . . . . . . . . . . . . . . . . . . . . . . . 135
4:1. . . . . . . . . . . . . . . . . . . . . . . . . . . . . . . . 25
11:2. . . . . . . . . . . . . . . . . . . . . . . . . . . . . . . 106
11:14. . . . . . . . . . . . . . . . . . . . . . . . . . . . . . 218
16:22. . . . . . . . . . . . . . . . . . . . . . . . . . . . . . 221
23:13–14. . . . . . . . . . . . . . . . . . . . . . . . . . . . . 83
27:9. . . . . . . . . . . . . . . . . . . . . . . . . . . . . . . 96
30:5. . . . . . . . . . . . . . . . . . . . . . . . . . . . . . . 230

Ecclesiastes

3:1, 6. . . . . . . . . . . . . . . . . . . . . . . . . . . . . . . 10
5:12. . . . . . . . . . . . . . . . . . . . . . . . . . . . . . . 112
8:15. . . . . . . . . . . . . . . . . . . . . . . . . . . . . . . 171
9:9–10. . . . . . . . . . . . . . . . . . . . . . . . . . . . . . 176

Isaiah

6:3. . . . . . . . . . . . . . . . . . . . . . . . . . . . . . . 242
41:13–14. . . . . . . . . . . . . . . . . . . . . . . . . . . . . 71
42:16. . . . . . . . . . . . . . . . . . . . . . . . . . . . . . . 55
53:4–5. . . . . . . . . . . . . . . . . . . . . . . . . . . . . . 64

Daniel

2:47. . . . . . . . . . . . . . . . . . . . . . . . . . . . . . . 144

Micah

    6:8 . . . . . . . . . . . . . . . . . . . . . . . . . . . . . . . . 151

Malachi

    2:10, 15 . . . . . . . . . . . . . . . . . . . . . . . . . . . . . 30

# NEW TESTAMENT

Matthew

    4:19 . . . . . . . . . . . . . . . . . . . . . . . . . . . . . . . 210

    6:33 . . . . . . . . . . . . . . . . . . . . . . . . . . . . . . . 141

    7:9 . . . . . . . . . . . . . . . . . . . . . . . . . . . . . . . . 207

    7:11 . . . . . . . . . . . . . . . . . . . . . . . . . . . . . . . 191

    7:9–11 . . . . . . . . . . . . . . . . . . . . . . . . . . . . . 179

    13:8–9 . . . . . . . . . . . . . . . . . . . . . . . . . . . . . 227

    18:10 . . . . . . . . . . . . . . . . . . . . . . . . . . . . . . . 86

    19:14 . . . . . . . . . . . . . . . . . . . . . . . . . . . . . . 236

    23:23 . . . . . . . . . . . . . . . . . . . . . . . . . . . . . . . 13

    25:37–40 . . . . . . . . . . . . . . . . . . . . . . . . . . . . 224

    26:39 . . . . . . . . . . . . . . . . . . . . . . . . . . . . . . 233

Mark

    10:13–14 . . . . . . . . . . . . . . . . . . . . . . . . . . . . 204

Luke

    12:15 . . . . . . . . . . . . . . . . . . . . . . . . . . . . . . 185

    18:13 . . . . . . . . . . . . . . . . . . . . . . . . . . . . . . 200

John

    13:34 . . . . . . . . . . . . . . . . . . . . . . . . . . . . . . 39

    21:25 . . . . . . . . . . . . . . . . . . . . . . . . . . . . 239

Romans

    12:6–8 . . . . . . . . . . . . . . . . . . . . . . . . . . . . . 36

1 Corinthians

    11:1 . . . . . . . . . . . . . . . . . . . . . . . . . . . . . 159

    12:4–6 . . . . . . . . . . . . . . . . . . . . . . . . . . . . 42

Ephesians

    4:25 . . . . . . . . . . . . . . . . . . . . . . . . . . . . . . 58

    5:8 . . . . . . . . . . . . . . . . . . . . . . . . . . . . . . . 19

    5:25 . . . . . . . . . . . . . . . . . . . . . . . . . . . . . . 80

    6:10–11 . . . . . . . . . . . . . . . . . . . . . . . . . . . 77

Philippians

    2:5–8 . . . . . . . . . . . . . . . . . . . . . . . . . . . . 213

    2:6–7 . . . . . . . . . . . . . . . . . . . . . . . . . . . . 121

Colossians

    4:6 . . . . . . . . . . . . . . . . . . . . . . . . . . . . . . 102

1 Timothy

    6:10 . . . . . . . . . . . . . . . . . . . . . . . . . . . . . 126

Hebrews

    2:17 . . . . . . . . . . . . . . . . . . . . . . . . . . . . . . 93

10:24–25............................... 33
10:36................................. 182
12:11................................. 216

James

1:2........................... 132, 165
1:17................................. 188
1:26.................................. 16
2:1................................. 154

1 Peter

2:24.................................. 61